RISING
ABOVE
Teen Devotional
FOR Girls

Khia Glover, LCSW

RISING ABOVE

Teen Devotional FOR Girls

**PRAYERS AND ACTIVITIES TO HELP
MANAGE ANXIETY**

ZEITGEIST • NEW YORK

Published in the United States by Zeitgeist Young Adult, an imprint of Zeitgeist™, a division of Penguin Random House LLC, New York.

penguinrandomhouse.com

Zeitgeist™ is a trademark of Penguin Random House LLC

Scripture quotations are taken from *The Message: The Bible in Contemporary Language.* Copyright © by Eugene H. Peterson 1993, 1994, 1995, 1996, 2000, 2001, 2002. Used by permission of NavPress. All rights reserved. Represented by Tyndale House Publishers Inc.

ISBN: 9780593435991
Ebook ISBN: 9780593690505

Author photograph © by Jaleccia Ates Photography
Cover and interior art © Shutterstock/knstartstudio
Cover design by Aimee Fleck
Interior design by Erin Yeung and Katy Brown
Edited by Kim Suarez and Caroline Lee

Printed in the United States of America

1 3 5 7 9 10 8 6 4 2

First Edition

For my heart, Dj. I am so blessed to be in your life. You have been through so much, but you haven't let it keep you down. You are a phenomenal, caring person, and I love you with all my heart.
—Momma Khia

CONTENTS

Introduction

Sometimes just being a girl causes anxiety, and that's on top of everyday stressors that teens face. Teen girls often think, *Am I pretty enough? Am I smart enough? Am I good enough?* While the pressure of being a teen can feel overwhelming and hard, these bouts of worry and stress are temporary and just a part of so-called growing pains for a lot of teenagers.

For others, though, anxious feelings aren't just momentary or fleeting. Some people battle with unrelenting anxiety that seems to follow them wherever they go.

True anxiety extends beyond being worried or nervous. Often a combination of fear and stress, anxiety can be debilitating for a teen. When someone experiences this kind of lasting anxiety, their thoughts and emotions—and even their entire body— are impacted. The physical exhaustion and mental chaos can become major roadblocks in school and in important relation- ships with friends and family.

Sometimes you don't even know where the anxiety is coming from, and that is probably the scariest part. It's hard to get over something, let alone explain it to someone else, when you don't even know what it is.

If any of the above seems familiar, you are not alone. Anxiety is very common and affects nearly 1 in 3 teens in America. The good news is that anxiety disorders are totally treatable.

For myself, I began experiencing anxiety and depression as a child. I firmly believe God didn't want suffering or pain for me, but he had a purpose. He helped me to overcome the worst of it, which led to my calling to help young people, like my teen self, who have severe anxiety.

In this book, I'll share 52 weekly devotions featuring Scripture that speaks to anxiety, worries, stress, and fears. The devotions will lead you to take the hand that God—your loving, caring God who is the only one who really knows and understands what you're going through—is holding out to you. You'll also find simple anxiety relief exercises proven to help manage symptoms. Some of these exercises are used more than once when they fit particularly well with a topic. You'll learn to use these skills in the moment to lessen or avoid the symptoms of anxiety.

Over the space of one year, you can gain understanding and the ability to improve your symptoms. No one can know if your anxiety will go away completely or forever. However, you can learn skills to reduce how often it happens, how long it lasts, and how intense it gets.

With God at your side, you can rise above anything, including anxiety.

How to Use This Book

When I got my first devotional, I didn't know what to expect or where to begin. This book was written to be both practical and inspirational and, most important, easy to read and use. Each weekly devotion takes just a few minutes to go through: beginning with a Bible verse, then a meaningful topic, and ending with a prayer. It's simple while also amazingly uplifting.

The book is divided into two parts. Part 1 has 52 weeks of devotions and Part 2 includes anxiety relief exercises. Each week's devotion comes with one suggested exercise (from Part 2) to learn and practice. The more you practice and internalize the skills from these exercises, the easier it will be to manage, soothe, and ease symptoms when you experience them.

Together, the devotions and exercises will help you find true relief so you can rise above anxiety and refocus on God and his beautiful plans for your life.

Part 1

The
Devotions

ANXIETY VERSUS FEAR

Let petitions and praises shape your worries into prayers, letting God know your concerns.
PHILIPPIANS 4:6

Did you know that anxiety and fear are different? Fear is a biological response to perceived danger and it energizes the body to move to safety. Anxiety is an emotional response that churns up when we are not able to express our emotions and needs. Anxiety is more a reaction to our pushed-down emotions about danger rather than a response to immediate danger around us.

With fear, we feel insecure for a moment, until a danger has passed. With anxiety, we feel insecure and nervous all the time—especially when there's something that makes us feel afraid or worried. Anxiety can impact our ability to do normal activities.

For instance, you may not want to leave your home because you're anxious about what might happen to you when you go outside. You might miss school because your anxiety makes you feel unsafe. Your anxiety may get in the way of your relationships and prevent you from enjoying time with your friends.

But know this: God invites you to turn "your worries into prayers, letting God know your concerns." He knows—and understands—what you're going through, and he wants you to be free from the worries that hold you back. He can help you overcome anxiety and empower you. Can you think of a worry you can give up to God?

Anxiety Relief Activity

Anxiety-Attack Safety Plan (page 120). Develop (and then keep with you) a one-page safety plan for sudden and severe anxiety attacks. Having a safety plan will make it easier for you to manage your symptoms in the moment. Consider sharing a copy of your plan with a close, trusted friend or family member, because there may be times you feel too overwhelmed to manage the panic attack on your own.

Prayer

God, thank you for knowing and understanding what I'm going through. Help me get free of the anxiety that has held me back. Amen.

ANXIETY FROM TRAUMA

"Don't panic. I'm with you. There's no need to fear, for I'm your God. I'll give you strength. I'll help you. I'll hold you steady, keep a firm grip on you."
ISAIAH 41:10

Anxiety is rooted in fears, but it is much more than the fear of spiders or being nervous about speaking to a crowd. Often, anxiety is not tied to *anything* apparent. Some days you just wake up anxious and have no idea why.

A more extreme form of anxiety can develop after experiencing trauma. For example, being in a serious car accident, witnessing a tragic event, losing a loved one, or being the victim of abuse. Anxiety caused by a traumatic experience is often diagnosed as post-traumatic stress disorder (PTSD). A person with PTSD may startle at loud noises, react strongly to accidental touch, and avoid people and situations that prompt memories of the traumatic event. If you think you may have PTSD and your symptoms are severe and disruptive to your everyday life, it's important to find a trauma therapist to help you recover.

Whether or not your anxiety is connected to a specific experience, God promises to be with you and to help you. You do not have to be strong on your own. You can lean on him. He will give you strength.

Anxiety Relief Activity

5 Senses, or 5-4-3-2-1 (page 122). When your anxiety and emotions are on overload, and even if you're dissociating (when it feels like you are outside of your body or watching yourself live), this simple activity will guide you to use your five senses to help calm you and bring your mind and body back into reality. You should then feel more grounded and think more clearly.

Prayer

God, thank you for upholding me when I don't have the strength to stand on my own. Help me regain a healthy, balanced life. Amen.

EFFECTS OF STRESS ON ANXIETY

No test or temptation that comes your way is beyond the course of what others have had to face. All you need to remember is that God will never let you down; he'll never let you be pushed past your limit; he'll always be there to help you come through it.

1 CORINTHIANS 10:13

What is the connection between anxiety and stress? Anxiety happens when stress becomes too much for our bodies and minds to hold. Some adults say that teens can't have stress because they're young and don't have many responsibilities outside of school. But the truth is, teenagers experience stress, and a lot of it.

Your body is changing. You're discovering new feelings. Learning about yourself. Dealing with the stress of grades. Preparing for your future. Peer pressure. Pressures from social media. Not to mention balancing time with friends, family, school, church, and maybe even a job. There is a lot on your plate.

God promises that he won't give you more than you can handle. That might not be the most comforting thing to hear, especially when a situation feels overwhelming. But God will help you overcome big challenges in your life, and the grace and wisdom he gives you will fuel you to continue conquering difficult moments.

Ask God for help when you need it. "He'll always be there to help you come through it."

Anxiety Relief Activity

Body Scan (page 124). When we experience anxiety, our bodies alert us in different ways. By completing a mental body scan from the bottoms of our feet to the top of our heads, we learn how and what our bodies are communicating to us. By becoming practiced at body scans, we can learn to recognize and tend to our early symptoms.

Prayer

Thank you, God, for getting me through all the hard experiences I've endured. I am blessed knowing that you'll always get me through the tough times. Amen.

THE IMPACT OF EMOTIONAL TRIGGERS

I'm an open book to you; even from a distance, you know what I'm thinking.
PSALM 139:2

Triggers are circumstances or events that send our anxiety into high gear. They can be sounds, smells, or a person who reminds us of something or someone that upset us.

Many triggers start as painful emotional events experienced through one or more of the five senses. Maybe a certain food made you horribly sick, and ever since then, smelling it or seeing it instantly stirs up stressful feelings. Why something becomes a trigger is not always clear. And not knowing why something triggers you doesn't make it easy to explain to others.

This verse tells us that God knows and understands everything about us, even the thoughts we can't seem to put into words. We can go to him to be understood. "I'm an open book to you; even from a distance, you know what I'm thinking." From that one sentence, one can be amazed, relieved, and thankful for a comforting God.

Recognize your triggers so the awareness can help prevent anxious responses. And if you can't explain your reaction to someone else, God still gets it.

Anxiety Relief Activity

Gradual Muscle Relaxation (page 126). Stress stores itself in your body and can cause stiffness and tension. Muscle relaxation not only helps your body, but also eases your mind.

Prayer

Lord, I am thankful that you know me so well. Help me recognize my triggers better so that they no longer cause me anxiety. Amen.

INVOLUNTARY RESPONSES TO FEAR

When I get really afraid, I come to you in trust.
PSALM 56:3

Have you heard of the body's *fight*, *flight*, or *freeze* responses to fear? These responses can happen whenever our bodies sense danger or stress, in any type of situation.

Let's say you're 16, and it's time for your big driving test. You practiced and are excited, but also jittery and nervous. You're not sure how you'll perform on demand and even wonder if you've practiced enough.

The *fight* response would be to take the test despite your anxiety. You might be *fleeing* if you're skipping the test because you're suddenly feeling sick. Or you might *freeze* up, forget everything you practiced, and blank out in the middle of the exam.

You may feel disappointed when your body responds in these ways, and you have no control over the reaction. But remember, these responses are totally normal and involuntary. They are ways your body tries to protect itself. Don't feel embarrassed if one of them happens to you.

Your initial reaction doesn't have to be the only response. You can pause, pray, and trust God to help you move through and beyond your anxiety. "When I get really afraid, I come to you in trust."

Anxiety Relief Activity

Get Moving (page 128). When you have anxiety you can't get rid of, or you feel your body beginning a fight, flight, or freeze response to an intensely stressful person or situation, moving your body—even in a small way—can start getting that stress out of you, allowing you to go to a safe place or push forward and complete your tasks.

Prayer

Creator, please remind me to pause and pray anytime I need help. Lead me through my anxiety. Don't let it stop me. Amen.

TAKING YOUR BRAIN OFF THE HAMSTER WHEEL

We use our powerful God-tools for . . . fitting every loose thought and emotion and impulse into the structure of life shaped by Christ.
2 CORINTHIANS 10:5

You have so many different thoughts swirling through your head that you can't focus on a single one. Your brain goes from trying to remember if you turned off your straightener, to whether you finished your homework assignment, to suddenly recalling that embarrassing moment from the third grade that you're sure everyone remembers—all in a moment. Your brain is on a hamster wheel.

Breathe. Breathe again. Call for Jesus to quiet your mind. Let him know the high-speed thoughts are too much to handle.

Then focus on *now*. Not the future, not the past. Only *now*. Breathe. Breathe again. Next, take one thought at a time. Third grade doesn't matter right now, so cut that thought away. Breathe. Breathe again. Okay, what does matter right now? Your straightener? Your homework assignment? Take a moment and take care of anything that needs urgent attention, as best you can. Remind yourself that it's okay and that mistakes can happen.

You get the idea.

Deep breathing and focusing on *now* are two powerful God-tools for "fitting every loose thought and emotion and impulse" into calmness. Prayer is another. When your thoughts zoom, Jesus will ease them. He doesn't want you to have stress at the heart of your life. He wants you to have an anxiety-free life, with him at the heart of your life.

Anxiety Relief Activity

Brain Dump (page 130). Dumping all of your thoughts on paper will help get your brain off the hamster wheel, allowing you to process one thought at a time, slowly and clearly.

Prayer

Jesus, please ease my thoughts when I'm unable to on my own. Then help me calm my breathing and prioritize what matters. Amen.

RELIEF FROM REPETITIVE THOUGHTS

A hostile world! I call to God, I cry to God to help me. From his palace he hears my call; my cry brings me right into his presence—a private audience!
PSALM 18:6

Do you remember the last time your mind had a worry on repeat, just like an annoying song that won't leave your head? Maybe you've had anxious thoughts that start with *I just can't* . . . Or maybe the thought on repeat was something a person said to you in passing.

Also known as *ruminating thoughts*, these thought loops can become a problem when we don't interrupt and reroute them. We'll begin to believe the worries, even if they aren't true. Ruminating thoughts are a big distraction. They take energy away from our ability to be successful throughout the day. A good way to stop ruminating thoughts is to interject with an entirely new thought or activity as a distraction, like journaling.

Psalm 18:6 reminds us we can call out to God in any distress that we have, even when we're mentally ambushed by untrue thoughts. Even more amazing is, "From his palace he hears my call; my cry brings me right into his presence—a private audience!"

What would your prayerful cry to God sound like?

Anxiety Relief Activity

Journal Your Feelings (page 132). Using a journal (or notebook) daily can quiet repetitive thoughts and help situations make more sense. Allowing your brain to freely express itself on paper can make a difference. You can even make some of your journal entries "letters to God."

Prayer

Lord, help me stop unhelpful thoughts by focusing on you and your great love for me. Help remind me that there's no better thought to think. Amen.

WHEN NO ONE ELSE UNDERSTANDS YOUR ANXIETY

Live carefree before God; he is most careful with you.
1 PETER 5:7

Anxiety makes even the most common tasks seem enormous. Making a phone call (even to someone you've known forever), driving, or turning in an assignment can all seem terrifying. But what can be even more isolating is feeling misunderstood when you try to explain your anxiety to someone. And it *is* hard to explain. You barely understand it yourself.

Anxiety is not logical, and when you're anxious, your brain can struggle to hold on to basic coping skills such as thinking clearly and logically. This is especially true when it seems impossible to shift out of a thought pattern or perspective that isn't helping you. You might feel a little wacky as a result. But rest assured, you'll be okay.

God cares about everything that concerns you. Even when people don't understand, he does. He made you. When you feel alone because you can't talk to your friends, or your family looks at you like you've got two heads, know that God understands completely. He wants you to talk to him about everything that makes you anxious and nervous, even if it sounds jumbled.

Will you bring everything that is making you anxious and nervous to God?

Anxiety Relief Activity

Speak to Your Inner Child (page 134). Some people who struggle with anxiety may have had experiences during childhood that made them feel unsafe. Some remember the event that caused their insecurity, but they don't realize that the incident caused ongoing feelings of anxiety. Some memories and experiences may not yet be clear to you. Talking with your scared inner child can help them to feel secure and protected.

Prayer

God, I am so grateful you understand me and that you know me inside and out. Thank you for helping me understand my anxiety. Amen.

FINDING HELP FOR PANIC ATTACKS

Take good counsel and accept correction—that's the way to live wisely and well.
PROVERBS 19:20

I experienced my first *major* panic attack in college. While walking from class to my dorm, I suddenly felt a shortness of breath that was different from my asthma. I was terrified. My heart beat faster, and everything felt blurry.

Later, I tried to remember when I first started to feel anxiety as a child. I was able to recall a time I had to participate in an oratorical (speaking) contest. On the way to the contest, I felt terrified to go onstage. I was hyperventilating, snapping at my mom any time she tried to be helpful (sorry, Mom), and I felt nauseous. At the time, I had no idea it was anxiety. If I had known, I may have been able to get professional help or learned how to better manage my feelings.

Getting support for your symptoms is *never* a bad thing. It also doesn't mean that you don't trust God to help you—God often works through people around us ("Take good counsel"). If you seek help, it is not a sign of weakness. Sometimes we need a little support from others, and that is perfectly okay. It's even wise.

Anxiety Relief Activity

Speak to a Therapist (page 136). Consider whether you might like to talk with a therapist. God created therapists, like me, just like he uses doctors, nurses, teachers, and other professionals in their work to help others. A therapist can teach you skills for managing anxiety symptoms and other unwanted feelings you might be experiencing. Therapists can also help you get to the root of your anxiety.

Prayer

God, please help me find trustworthy relationships to guide me through my anxiety and fears. Lead them to help me with your wisdom. Amen.

PANIC ATTACKS AFFECT THE BODY

My life is well and whole, secure in the middle of danger, even while thousands are lined up against me.
PSALM 55:18

Some of the hardest battles we'll ever struggle with will be the ones in our minds. Anxiety can be terrifying and taxing on the mind and body. When anxious thoughts consume us, it's a challenge to put a stop to the negative thinking.

You may have had the unfortunate experience of someone calling you "dramatic" or saying you were "overreacting" during an anxiety attack. People who've experienced panic attacks have gone to the hospital believing they were having heart attacks. Anxiety can cause both panic and physical pain.

Whenever I read this verse from Psalm 55, I identify with the feeling that "thousands are lined up against me," especially when family and friends don't understand. But the verse assures me that "my life is . . . secure in the middle of danger."

You're secure because God protects you, even when your mind feels like it's going to war against itself. This is not a losing battle. Every time you get through an anxiety or panic attack, you are victorious! You win. Every time.

Anxiety Relief Activity

Belly Breaths (page 138). If you're having a panic attack, the first line of defense is to slow your breathing with belly breaths. Regulating your breathing will send a message to your brain that you are safe. The second line of defense is to secure yourself. After belly breathing, use the "5 Senses, or 5-4-3-2-1" technique (page 122) to help bring your mind and body back into reality.

Prayer

Lord, please help me fight the battles of my mind and to ultimately recover from anxiety. Amen.

STRATEGIES FOR ANXIETY RELIEF

These hard times are small potatoes compared to the coming good times, the lavish celebration prepared for us.
2 CORINTHIANS 4:17

Sixty seconds of an anxiety attack can feel like six days. But, as many times as you have anxiety in a day, a week, a year, or for however long it lasts, remember you can always seek and surrender it to God.

I wish I could tell you that one day you'll wake up and never experience anxiety again, but only God knows the ultimate plan for you. All things are possible with God, but it's in his plan and timing to determine what he has for us.

I do have confidence that your feelings of panic or anxiety will ease *and* last for shorter and shorter periods of time. Relief will come.

And whenever your anxiety isn't present, live your life to the fullest. Rejoice in those moments, praising God.

When anxious moments arrive, slow down, take care of yourself, do some activities in this book to relieve your symptoms, pray, and remind yourself that it won't last forever. God is right there with you to comfort you. And he will still be there after the anxiety passes.

Anxiety Relief Activity

Sit with Your Emotions (page 140). When we're anxious, emotions can seem to come at us from every direction, making it difficult to know what we're even feeling. When we sit with our emotions for a few minutes, we might be able to understand what's going on inside and where our feelings might be coming from.

Prayer

God, thank you for reminding me that even my toughest moments and situations are temporary. Please give me strength to get through each one. Amen.

IDENTIFY ANXIOUS THOUGHTS

Summing it all up, friends, I'd say you'll do best by filling your minds and meditating on things true, noble, reputable, authentic, compelling, gracious—the best, not the worst; the beautiful, not the ugly; things to praise, not things to curse.

PHILIPPIANS 4:8

Sometimes my anxious thoughts go wild. I freak out about everything, even with a task I've done a thousand times! Has this ever happened to you?

This typically starts with something like: *I'm horrible at taking tests!* Then, you start to feel nervous about the upcoming test. Next, you'll avoid studying, or you'll overthink your answers during the test. People with anxiety have a lot of similar thoughts running through their minds.

Next time you catch negative thoughts, ask yourself, *What is the* truth? You may be someone who struggles with taking tests, to continue our example, but that doesn't mean you can't do it or that you're horrible at it.

So, redirect your thoughts: *Tests are difficult for me, but I've worked hard studying. I know I can do this.* By changing your perspective, you can change your circumstances and ease your mind and body. Kind self-talk will help you slow down and think more clearly.

The thoughts we tell ourselves can be very powerful. We can ease our minds by "meditating on things true . . . compelling, gracious—the best . . . the beautiful . . . things to praise."

Anxiety Relief Activity

Audio Journaling (page 142). Try speaking your thoughts into the voice notes on your phone. You might start venting or talking about negative feelings you're experiencing. We're often told that we shouldn't voice negative thoughts, but sometimes we need to hear ourselves to see how anxious we are or how ridiculously hard we're being on ourselves. After, speak some positive truths about yourself or the situation.

Prayer

God, help me focus my thoughts on things that are "true, noble, reputable, authentic, compelling, gracious." Help me think clearly and feel better. Amen.

THINK BEAUTIFUL TRUTHS

Watch the way you talk . . . Say only what helps, each word a gift.
EPHESIANS 4:29

A thought enters my head: *I'm a failure. I don't deserve to have friends or success.*

I might not actually believe this at first. But, if I don't correct that thought, it will begin to resonate, and I'll eventually start to believe it.

Intrusive thoughts usually go hand in hand with anxiety. They are called *intrusive* because they're not intended and are disruptive.

Catch and identify these thoughts as early as possible so you don't start to believe the negative talk. When I believed the thoughts, my behaviors began to adapt to those words. I started to push family and friends away and my grades dropped because my intrusive thoughts told me I wasn't good enough.

So, pay attention to what your mind is saying to you. If it's telling you something negative about yourself, then it's probably not true, because God made you to be amazing.

Recognize intrusive thoughts, stop them, and tell yourself the positive truth. *I do deserve friends and success. I am trying my best. God has an amazing plan for my life.*

"Watch the way you talk" and think. "Say only what helps, each word a gift."

Anxiety Relief Activity

Conquering Intrusive Thoughts (page 144). Sneaky, intrusive thoughts try to prove us wrong about ourselves. You can conquer intrusive thoughts by choosing to think the opposite. For instance, if you're thinking, *What if I fail?* conquer that by thinking, *What if I succeed?* Positive thinking frees up your imagination to come up with ideas that can lead you to much better outcomes.

Prayer

Lord, help me to think more positively about myself. Help me remember that I have the power to change my thoughts. Amen.

MAKING MISTAKES?
GIVE YOURSELF GRACE

So let's walk right up to him and get what he is so ready to give. Take the mercy, accept the help.
HEBREWS 4:16

I can be very hard on myself, the same way I'm sure you can be hard on yourself. Making even one mistake, or feeling like I didn't do something well enough, can send me into a cycle of anxiety for days (also known as *ruminating*).

But in these moments, I remind myself that I have to give myself grace, the same way I would be gracious and compassionate to a friend who made a mistake. I also have to remember that everybody makes mistakes.

If God believes I'm worthy of grace, or forgiveness, for my mistakes, then who am I to say that I don't deserve to show myself the same grace?

Hebrews 4:16 tells us to be bold about receiving grace and mercy from God. We should also be bold about giving mercy—to others and to ourselves.

So give yourself some grace today. Assess areas where you can improve in your life. Do any jump out to you now? Reflect on it lovingly, not with harsh judgment or criticism. You deserve kindness, and you deserve it most of all from yourself.

Anxiety Relief Activity

Reframing Thoughts (page 146). Negativity limits our confidence and ability to do or be more than what we currently believe. We can change our perspectives by reframing those negative thoughts to include positive statements and goals. This inspires the mind to find ways to push forward and achieve more. It also helps us to be kind and loving to ourselves.

Prayer

God, help me give myself grace as freely as you do. Help me to be kind and loving to myself and to others. Amen.

FINDING PEACE

"I've told you all this so that trusting me, you will be unshakable and assured, deeply at peace. In this godless world you will continue to experience difficulties. But take heart! I've conquered the world."
JOHN 16:33

The Bible speaks a lot about peace. But what is peace? Peace is not the absence of anxiety. Peace doesn't mean being worry-free. Instead, peace is what you experience when you're anxious and worried but decide to surrender the weight of worrying and the problem that is bothering you.

Peace happens when you're in the shower, crying because you're so overwhelmed, feeling lost, terrified, clueless about how you're going to get through it all, and yet saying, "God, I release this to you," and letting it go. Peace is freedom.

Peace is like insurance for when something bad happens, like a car wreck or house fire. Insurance doesn't make the situation less devastating; it promises that someone will guide you to solve the problem. When we give our worries to God, he becomes our champion and figures out what's next.

Hard times happen to everyone, no matter how rich you are, where you live, or where you come from. No one is exempt. But Jesus has "conquered the world"—it's his; nothing is uncertain to him. So when we give our troubles to him, we find peace and hopefulness for what is to come, despite difficult times.

Anxiety Relief Activity

Gradual Exposure (page 148). It might feel more comfortable to wait until all fear is gone before you resume a normal, peaceful life, but that won't always leave you feeling satisfied. If you confront your fears, you can ultimately build confidence and trust in yourself. This week's activity will help you to move forward while also maintaining a sense of control.

Prayer

God, I want to have the assurance of peace during my storms. Help me find peace in you. Amen.

PERFECT PEACE COMES FROM GOD

Before you know it, a sense of God's wholeness, everything coming together for good, will come and settle you down. It's wonderful what happens when Christ displaces worry at the center of your life.
PHILIPPIANS 4:7

Have you ever had a big event you were preparing for, maybe a performance or a school presentation, but instead of stressing, you felt very calm? You're probably always aware of lurking anxiety, so you might have felt a little suspicious at your calmness.

This is the peace of God.

The peace of God does not follow any human logic. *How could I possibly feel calm and peaceful with all these pressures?* When Paul wrote to the Philippians, he described the peace of God as "a sense of God's wholeness, everything coming together for good" that "will come and settle you down." Wow. Peace is a blessing straight from God and confirms that you are going in the direction that God has laid out for you.

Peace "happens when Christ displaces worry at the center of your life." Trust in Jesus that he'll get you through everything that comes your way. If he brings you to it, he will bring you through it. When you have that much trust in Jesus, you experience more and more of God's peace.

Anxiety Relief Activity

Visualization Brings Better Outcomes (page 150). Jesus plans for you to be successful in many aspects of your life. Visualizing good experiences can help you focus more on the positive possibilities than the negative. This can help feed better outcomes in reality, just as God intended.

Prayer

God, help me trust Jesus with absolutely everything that comes into my life, so I experience more and more of your peace. Amen.

MARVELOUSLY MADE

Oh yes, you shaped me first inside, then out; you formed me in my mother's womb. I thank you, High God—you're breathtaking! Body and soul, I am marvelously made! I worship in adoration—what a creation!
PSALM 139:13–14

During our teen years, sometimes just being a girl causes anxiety. We often think, *Am I pretty enough? Am I smart enough? Am I good enough?* We compare ourselves to others. We obsess over our clothes and hairstyle. The pressure can be overwhelming.

But God shaped you "inside, then out," to be "marvelously made." God made every single part of you with intention. He personally chose your appearance, your intellect, and your abilities. God designed you to be more than pretty enough and more than smart enough. You have what it takes!

You can be confident that he made you for a special purpose. It's absolutely okay to get your nails done, practice the hottest makeup trends, and style your hair all cute. But know that when God made you, he had so much more in mind for you.

When you begin to get anxious about being perfect, keep in mind that God already sees you as perfect. Yes, we want others to see us as beautiful and smart—acknowledgment and acceptance from our peers are important. But know that God sees you as your best self. Let that confidence and inner light shine through!

Anxiety Relief Activity

Positive Affirmations (page 152). Affirmations are positive truths you repeat to yourself. They pump you up and remind you of who you are and what you're capable of doing. Affirmations can help relieve your anxiety and doubts.

Prayer

God, thank you for creating me to be special. Help me to remember that you have made each and every one of us uniquely and beautifully. Help me be confident in the wonderful, marvelous way you made me. Amen.

HE LOVES THAT TOO!

You're beautiful from head to toe . . . beautiful beyond compare,
absolutely flawless.
SONG OF SONGS 4:7

Anxiety distracts us from appreciating all our amazing and wonderful qualities. Instead, we focus on our flaws, inadequacies, and insecurities. Anxiety reminds us of all the things we dislike about ourselves, making us doubt ourselves and our abilities. We believe its lies that no one will love us, or even like us.

But God sees *no* flaws in you. In his eyes, you are "beautiful beyond compare." He made you perfectly, and he made you unique. What parts of yourself are you proud of?

The quirks and characteristics you just can't stand about yourself . . . God loves that about you. The shape of your nose? Yep, he loves that! The way you stutter when you get excited? He loves that too! That birthmark you try to cover with makeup? He adores that about you! The way you get so upset and irritable when you're anxious? He loves you through that, and he is so proud of you for working on it so diligently.

What if you can learn to love these qualities and even use them for God's glory? Ask him and he will help you.

Anxiety Relief Activity

Connect with Your Love Language (page 154). Discovering and responding to your love language can fill a void of love that your heart and spirit may feel is missing. It's one of the best ways to help yourself feel loved.

> **Prayer**
>
> Lord, thank you for loving me just as I am. Help me love the qualities you gave me and use them for your glory. Amen.

NO ONE COMPARES TO YOU

Make a careful exploration of who you are and the work you have been given, and then sink yourself into that. Don't be impressed with yourself. Don't compare yourself with others.
GALATIANS 6:4

Scrolling through social media apps, like YouTube or TikTok, do you ever browse other people's accounts and then compare what they have with what you *don't* have? Material things, like a car or house; achievements, like winning awards or being selected by a recruiter; or physical characteristics, like your hair-style? The life you thought was okay suddenly seems dull and worthless.

We've all had moments like this, even these seemingly perfect people we compare ourselves to. Scripture reminds us to pay attention to what we're doing in our own lives.

What abilities has God given you? How has he blessed you to be unique? God already made you perfect for the tasks he has planned. When you compare yourself to others, you can lose sight of your own dreams and goals.

Maybe you didn't even care about having a certain item or feel you were missing out until you saw a suggested post. Focus on feeling gratitude for what you have going for you and if necessary, consider taking a break from social media. Celebrate the special plans God has prepared for your present and future. Don't allow toxic comparisons to crush your achievements and goals. You are unique. No one compares to you!

Anxiety Relief Activity

Creative Expression (page 156). Pain can often bring out beautiful creative expressions. And these creative expressions bring healing. It doesn't matter what form of art you choose: poetry, drawing, painting, music, dance, and so forth. Whatever feels good to you, put your heart into it and begin to heal. Be uniquely you!

Prayer

God, you have blessed me with so much. I am so grateful. Help me stay focused on the work you've given me to do. Amen.

SENSORY SENSITIVITY?
FIND SOLITUDE.

You're my place of quiet retreat; I wait for your Word to renew me.
PSALM 119:114

A common symptom of anxiety, *sensory sensitivity* is when you are overstimulated and irritable. Noises seem louder, your clothes feel uncomfortable, and the slightest touch sends you into overload.

In these moments, find solitude and turn inward to God for refuge. Often, all that is needed is a feeling of safety, and that can be hard to find with others. God provides safety and recenters your heart. You might feel close to him when reading a few of David's psalms. David often felt overwhelmed himself and found that God was his "place of quiet retreat." As you read and wait for God's "Word to renew," you'll feel the noise melting away and your body, mind, and spirit easing back to a place of serenity.

Solitude can be a dedicated time to spend with God. We might be apart from all other people, but our loving God is always with us. Designate quiet time with God, and he will provide a retreat so your strength is renewed. Which psalms help you feel close to God? Do you have a place you can go to feel safe? Where can you retreat when you need quiet?

Anxiety Relief Activity

Change Your Environment (page 158). Creating a space—or changing up the space you currently have—whether big or small, can be transforming. Make your space one where you can be creative and relaxed, and do whatever it is you need for that moment. No matter how you're feeling, you'll have a designated space just for you . . . and God.

Prayer

Thank you, God, for being my refuge. Thank you for the safety I am able to find in you. Amen.

AFTER AN ANXIETY ATTACK, YOU NEED REST

At day's end I'm ready for sound sleep, for you, God, have put my life back together.
PSALM 4:8

When your body starts to calm down from a sudden onset of anxiety, you might not feel motivated to do activities that usually excite you. You may find yourself crying more than usual, sleeping more, sleeping less, eating less (or more) than usual, or not wanting to see friends. Feeling depressed can happen because anxiety symptoms are physically exhausting. They cause a cycle of symptoms that are overwhelming.

"Force yourself to get up and do something" might be a familiar phrase you've heard. But it's okay to let your body rest. Especially after a period of anxiety, your body might be signaling to you that it needs to slow down and recover. Try not to shame yourself for taking time to reset.

After a couple of days, start moving around again a little. You don't want to get stuck after sinking low. Go easy and allow the peace of God to fill and comfort you, without shame. It is okay to slow down and rest. And to trust God while you do. "For you, God . . . put my life back together."

Anxiety Relief Activity

Sit with Your Emotions (page 140). When we're anxious, emotions can seem to come at us from every direction. It may be difficult to know what we're even feeling. When we sit with our emotions and let them flow, we might be able to see what's going on inside and where our feelings might be coming from. When we understand that, we can start to let go of the stress and anxiety. And we can rest.

Prayer

God, I don't understand everything I'm feeling, but I ask for your soothing comfort to fill me now, and I ask for time to rest. Amen.

HIDE, AND SEEK GOD

I'll contemplate [God's] beauty; I'll study at his feet. That's the only quiet, secure place in a noisy world, the perfect getaway, far from the buzz of traffic.
PSALM 27:4–5

Does anxiety ever make you want to run and hide? Your heart is racing, your breathing is heavy, and you begin to panic, trying to find the nearest place to shrink and disappear.

Sure, sometimes protecting yourself by hiding will give you the break you need before you jump back in and conquer what is scaring you. Should you hide forever? Nope.

In these moments, take a break and think about why you're experiencing the anxiety and try to identify other emotions (like feeling guilty, frustrated, or left out) that also may be rising in you. Then come up with a plan that uses small steps to conquer it (like praying before a hard conversation or deep breathing before you take an exam). Finally, seek God to help you reaffirm your abilities and gifts. "Study at his feet. That's the only quiet, secure place in a noisy world, the perfect getaway."

When you're ready to come out of hiding, stand boldly where God has called you to be. Stand tall with confidence. He is right beside you.

Anxiety Relief Activity

Heart Hug (page 160). During panic attacks, you may notice your heart beating faster and wish you could slow it down. You can. Use your hands to give yourself a heart hug from the outside. This can ease your anxiety, help clear your mind, and begin to restore some confidence. You might feel like you've been given a real hug, even if you're alone.

Prayer

God, please give me the strength to get back up and stand in confidence as the capable young woman you've created me to be. Amen.

RISE AND SHINE

It's useless to rise early and go to bed late, and work your worried fingers to the bone. Don't you know he enjoys giving rest to those he loves?
PSALM 127:2

We've all had those nights when we stayed up late to cram for a test or stayed awake worrying about something that might happen at school the next day. Sometimes my anxiety wakes me up before my alarm goes off. My thoughts are already running, thinking about everything I need to complete that day.

This verse reminds us that waking up early and staying awake late—because we're consumed with worry—is not helpful. How awful does it feel to start a new day filled with worry?

That's not what God wants for us. "Don't you know he enjoys giving rest to those he loves?" Take charge of your day knowing God cares about you, and that he wants you to take good care of yourself.

Allow yourself to sleep and rest, and give your brain and body a break to recover. Then you'll feel refreshed for the new day ahead.

Anxiety Relief Activity

Journal Your Feelings (page 132). Using a journal (or notebook) every day can help you process your thoughts better. It may be difficult to express your thoughts and feelings to someone out loud, but allowing your brain to freely express on paper may be easier for you. Try journaling a letter to God. If you've started journaling, keep it going. Many people journal throughout their lives and experience countless ongoing benefits—including better sleep.

Prayer

God, I give my problems to you so I don't miss sleep because of worry. Help me to enjoy your gift of rest. Amen.

WEEK
24

COMFORTING OTHERS WHO STRUGGLE

So speak encouraging words to one another. Build up hope so you'll all be together in this, no one left out, no one left behind. I know you're already doing this; just keep on doing it.
1 THESSALONIANS 5:11

When Kierra and I first started working together in therapy, she was nervous to admit that her mom was a big source of her anxiety. Kierra's mom also struggled with anxiousness. When Kierra's mom would experience stress, her speech would speed up, and she'd become more critical about things like the music playing too loudly or Kierra's clothes in the bathroom. It sent Kierra's anxiety into a spiral.

Kierra was afraid to have this conversation with her mom, because she wasn't sure how her mom would respond.

This verse reminds us that we need to speak comforting, encouraging words to one another. Like Kierra, if you have similar issues with your parents or anyone who triggers your anxiety, remember that Jesus wants us to speak kindly to each other and to comfort one another.

The anxious person who is causing your anxiety? Somebody else caused their anxiety too. We're all trying to get healthier emotions together.

Try having a conversation with the person who triggers you. If you aren't sure what to say, pray about it first. Ask God to help you be brave and kind.

Anxiety Relief Activity

Breathe In Confidence, Breathe Out Fear (page 162). Mindful breathing will help bring you back to your body and senses and keep you grounded, especially before a difficult conversation with someone.

Prayer

Lord, when I talk to my loved one about their impact on my anxiety, please give me strength and kind, comforting words to say. Amen.

FAMILY PRESSURES

Be gentle with one another, sensitive.
EPHESIANS 4:32

Family is a blessing, but some of us don't always have the best relationships with family members. Maybe they're not often gentle or sensitive to us. So, we might connect with a group of kindly people who we consider as family, even if we're not related to them.

Perhaps your family members just want the best for you and have the best intentions. But you might feel a lot of pressure from their expectations—to be who and what they want you to be, to succeed in the way they want you to succeed, and to please them. The weight of it all can be triggering.

In what ways do your family relationships impact you? If it's hard to honor their wishes and desires, think about ways to speak to them from your heart.

Pray for the courage to be vulnerable and honest with your family. Pray that God will guide you when to talk to them and give you the right words to say, so that you are gentle and sensitive to your family. And ask God to open their hearts to hear and comfort you. They might be more open and understanding than you expect.

Anxiety Relief Activity

Speak to a Therapist (page 136). Consider whether you might like to talk with a therapist. God created therapists, like me, just like he uses doctors, nurses, teachers, and other professionals in their work to help others. A therapist can teach you skills for managing anxiety symptoms you might be experiencing. Therapists can also help you get to the root of your anxiety and help families heal and support one another.

Prayer

God, thank you for my family. Please help us to be supportive of one another in ways that provide peace and love. Amen.

MENDING BROKEN RELATIONSHIPS

"Nothing, you see, is impossible with God."
LUKE 1:37

I had a client whose father walked out of her life when she was really young. Eventually, her dad wanted to come back into her life, and understandably she had a lot of anxiety around the possibility of reconnecting. When her dad would call, she would feel very anxious thinking about his motives. When they finally met and spent time together, it was never comfortable. It was difficult for my client to open her heart to him.

Is there a relationship you're thinking about repairing, maybe with a friend, family member, or another loved one?

In the Scripture above, God's angel says, "Nothing . . . is impossible with God." That includes mending a broken relationship—if it is God's will that it be mended.

It's normal to be nervous about being vulnerable and giving someone another chance. *What if they hurt me again?* While you might not be able to trust the person who hurt you, you can always put trust in God. He will lead you in the right direction.

Anxiety Relief Activity

Anxiety-Attack Safety Plan (page 120). Update (and then keep with you) your one-page safety plan for sudden and severe anxiety attacks. You've learned strategies to help you avoid or overcome panic attacks. Update any strategies, symptoms, contacts, and the like to help you manage when you feel overwhelmed in the moment. It might be helpful to share this updated copy of your plan with a close, trusted friend or family member, because at times you might feel too overwhelmed to manage the panic attack on your own.

Prayer

God, you know how much I love _____ (person's name). Fixing my relationship with them seems impossible. But please make it possible. Amen.

HANDLING GOSSIP

Be gracious in your speech. The goal is to bring out the best in others in a conversation, not put them down, not cut them out.
COLOSSIANS 4:6

Rumors, gossip, and high school seem to go hand in hand. Young people are often told not to worry about what others might say and think. But the truth is that it hurts and can stir anxious feelings in us.

Wanting to be accepted by your peers is normal. And it feels really uncomfortable to think about peers possibly talking about you and starting drama.

How do we handle it? The Bible tells us, "Be gracious in your speech." Gossip is hurtful to us, but we do not have to be hurtful back. We can be gracious and show them what decent people are like (check out Proverbs 25:21–22). That's what Jesus often did when people were vicious to him.

At the same time, we don't have to stand around and let gossip hurt us. (Jesus didn't always stick around either.) We can walk away and let distance be an ongoing barrier between us. A *boundary*. We should be gracious in our speech if we have to talk to a gossipy person—"not put them down, not cut them out"—but we can also respect ourselves enough to avoid them.

Anxiety Relief Activity

Set Healthy Boundaries (page 164). Setting boundaries for how you allow others to interact with you and how you interact with them will save you a lot of drama and heartache. If you're not used to putting up boundaries, doing so, especially at first, might feel foreign and almost mean, like an act of rejection, but boundaries are a basic form of protection. Healthy boundaries will help maintain peace, for yourself and for those around you.

Prayer

God, protect me from gossip. If I am compelled to speak, give me gracious words to say, or help me simply walk away. Amen.

HEALTHY LOVE FEELS SAFE

There is no room in love for fear. Well-formed love banishes fear. Since fear is crippling, a fearful life—fear of death, fear of judgment—is one not yet fully formed in love.
1 JOHN 4:18

Alexa is one of my clients. Alexa's boyfriend was mean to her, always making her doubt her worth. When she questioned if he was trustworthy, he made her feel crazed (also commonly known as *gaslighting*). Sometimes he would break up with her; sometimes he would just ignore her, causing her to worry and panic. Every time he behaved this way toward her, she would have breakdowns and panic attacks. Alexa felt like her whole world was ending in those moments.

This was not a healthy, loving relationship. Alexa and I worked together to determine what healthy relationships would look like for her.

This verse is specific about *perfect* love casting out fear. God's perfect love is the force that drives away any feelings of insecurity, uncertainty, fear, and any other feelings that can cause anxiety. We are safe with God.

We can apply this to all relationships. Healthy love is healing and helps us feel at ease. Healthy love doesn't cause anxiety or fear.

God's perfect love gives us confidence to love ourselves and others in ways that resemble his love for us—so people we care about feel safe with us.

Anxiety Relief Activity

Set Healthy Boundaries (page 164). When a relationship is causing you to feel uneasy and anxious, identify what a healthy relationship looks like to you. Work on setting healthy boundaries to make it easier to recognize when someone is unhealthy for you and walk away. This can be any kind of relationship—family, friends, romantic partners, or even certain habits. Set the standard of how people treat you. You are worthy of love and you should be treated with respect.

Prayer

God, help me to recognize and put distance in relationships and interactions that aren't healthy for me. Amen.

RECOVERING FROM HEARTBREAK

You called out to God in your desperate condition; he got you out in the nick of time. He quieted the wind down to a whisper, put a muzzle on all the big waves.
PSALM 107:28–29

There have been countless times in my life when my anxiety convinced me that I just wouldn't be able to go on. Especially when experiencing heartbreak—a breakup, a friendship ending, losing a loved one—everything can seem so dark. *How can I ever go on without this person in my life?*

You thought that you'd always be together. Now that you aren't, your stomach is in knots.

Once, I was driving past a gas station and saw my new boy-friend getting gas. I saw a girl I was suspicious about get in the passenger seat. Seeing them together, I knew in my gut it was over between us. I was so heartbroken!

I finally cried out to God, saying, "I don't want this memory to control me anymore!" It took me a long time before I was able to drive down that street again without that gut-wrenching feeling. But eventually, with time, I could drive past that gas station and feel okay.

Today's Scripture says, "You called out to God in your desperate condition . . . He quieted the wind down to a whisper." God will quiet your inner storms. He promises to bring you out of the darkness.

Anxiety Relief Activity

Creative Expression (page 156). Pain can often bring out beauty and creativity. These creative expressions are healing. It doesn't matter what form of art we choose. Whatever inspires you, use it to heal from whatever may be hurting you inside.

Prayer

God, I don't know how I will ever make it past this, but you can make it happen. Please help me find the light. Amen.

SEEKING OUT COMFORTING CONNECTIONS

When I was upset and beside myself, you calmed me down and cheered me up.

PSALM 94:19

Have you ever received a big hug that felt like it melted your problems away? Growing up, I knew two women, a mother and daughter at church, who gave *the best* hugs. If I felt anxious or down, I found one of them and hugged them. I could feel all my worries melt away.

Our anxiety often makes us want to pull back from others. It tricks us into thinking we're alone, but we're not.

Near you are people who can love and support you. It might not always be the people you expect, but God can place amazing people into your life. Keep your eyes open for trustworthy people, and you might find you are willing to open up to them. Maybe you don't feel comfortable sharing the exact worry. Neither woman at church ever asked me what was wrong. They just embraced me tightly and shared their love. But I had to be vulnerable enough to seek them out and let them know I needed comfort.

Being vulnerable is scary, especially when your anxiety makes it hard to trust others. But through good people, you can experience God calming you down and cheering you up.

Anxiety Relief Activity

Heart Hug (page 160). Heart hugs can ease your anxiety, help clear your mind, and begin to restore some confidence. In general, try to get and give hugs often from someone you trust, someone who makes you feel safe and loved.

Prayer

Lord, please place the right people in my life to support me through my fears and anxiety. Help me know who I can trust. Amen.

GOD'S GUIDANCE

By your words I can see where I'm going; they throw a beam of light on my dark path.
PSALM 119:105

A client once shared that her anxiety made it difficult to make decisions. She said every time she came to a conclusion, thoughts about why she shouldn't trust her decision—and the different and possibly better ways to decide—would fill her head.

Learning to trust yourself is a huge part of anxiety management. One way to build trust in yourself is to trust that God guides your path. "By your words I can see where I'm going; they throw a beam of light." Reading the Bible regularly will teach you to make good decisions.

Another way to build trust in yourself is to trust that you hear the Holy Spirit, which is always guiding you. The more you listen for the Holy Spirit's guidance and the closer you grow to God, the more clearly you will recognize his voice and direction.

What is God speaking into your heart today?

Anxiety Relief Activity

Decision Tree (page 166). Making decisions can seem challenging when your thoughts keep swirling in your head. Alleviate any stressors by making a decision tree and writing down all your thoughts, options, and possible outcomes. As you complete this activity, ask and listen for the Holy Spirit's guidance.

Prayer

Holy Spirit, thank you for guiding me and lighting my way. Help me to know your voice better and to follow where you lead. Amen.

DON'T BE AFRAID TO TRY

"Haven't I commanded you? Strength! Courage! Don't be timid; don't get discouraged. God, your God, is with you every step you take."
JOSHUA 1:9

Intimidation and fear of rejection—these anxious feelings can make life scary, especially when you want to try new things. Maybe you're afraid to go out for the varsity sports team, run for class president, or apply for college. On one hand, you believe you have the skills, but on the other hand, you have all the what-ifs. *What if I don't make it? What if I get rejected? What if they don't like me?* These questions are our doubts. Doubts can diminish our purpose.

Hear what God is saying: Have strength! Have courage! "God, your God, is with you every step you take." When you have a vision in your heart, it comes from God, and he already has the plan to see you through it.

Now, in life, there is always a risk that things might not work out the way you had in mind. But there is always a lesson, even in that. Sometimes God has an even bigger and better idea for you. Trust in God. Don't let intimidation or fear of rejection stop you. Be strong and courageous! Go for it! God will direct your wins. He is with you all the way.

Anxiety Relief Activity

Create a Vision Board (page 168). A vision board is a poster board with glued-on pictures that show whatever you want to achieve. I prefer using glue and paper so I can see it on my wall daily. You may choose to create your vision board on a computer using a program like Canva or Google Slides. You can even save it as your computer's background or screen saver so it is always in your view. Creating a vision board and placing it on your wall keeps your vision—your dreams and goals—in mind. Staying focused on your goals can help tame negative thoughts.

Prayer

Lord, make me strong and courageous. When you place wants and goals inside me, help me to pursue them with faith and not fear. Amen.

FROM DOUBTFUL TO DARING

"Be strong. Take courage. Don't be intimidated. Don't give them a second thought because God, your God, is . . . right there with you. He won't let you down; he won't leave you."
DEUTERONOMY 31:6

The popular buzz phrase "imposter syndrome" refers to the anxiety that comes from thinking that we're not qualified or good enough to do something and fearing that someone will find us out.

There are debates on whether "imposter syndrome" is real, but many people feel moments of inadequacy. For example, you've been selected as editor of your high school newspaper, but you're afraid someone might expose you to be unqualified because you got a C- on a standardized English Language Arts test a few years ago.

Even if you received C- grades on *20* ELA essays, that doesn't mean you're not qualified to be editor! It does mean that you'll have to continue working hard, just like you did to be given that role.

Deuteronomy 31 says, "Be strong. Take courage. Don't be intimidated." *Because God himself is with you.*

If you want something, go after it. Many people in the world who are excellent in their fields have felt they don't deserve to be there. Don't let what others might think hold you back. Be strong and courageous!

Anxiety Relief Activity

Visualization Brings Better Outcomes (page 159). Visualizing the great experiences you want to have for an upcoming event can help you focus more on the positive possibilities than the negative. This can help feed much better outcomes during the actual event.

Prayer

Jesus, help me become courageous in going after my heart's desires, without doubting my qualifications, regardless of what others might say or think. Amen.

PUTTING GOD IN CHARGE

Put God in charge of your work, then what you've planned will take place.
PROVERBS 16:3

Have you had moments where you question whether or not your efforts are worth your time and energy? Maybe you've been applying to colleges and haven't heard back yet. Maybe you've been working on a huge project or new idea, and it just doesn't seem to be going anywhere. When you're trying to be patient, anxiety can make you believe that all your hard work is a complete waste.

Whatever your goal is, "put God in charge of your work." In other words, depend completely on him. When you do, "then what you've planned will take place." He will either remove the challenges or get you past them. You might not know how it'll work out—sometimes God acts and reaches us through a person near us—but it will happen when you give it to him and keep going.

The app you want to develop? Put God in charge—depend completely on him. Becoming valedictorian? Put God in charge. Struggling to pass that hard class? Put God in charge.

Acknowledge your anxiety, use coping skills from this book to help relieve your symptoms, and push through, depending on God to make it happen.

Anxiety Relief Activity

Brain Break (page 170). When we trust God, we can find relief from a lot of our stress. But that doesn't mean we can just stop doing our part. We have to push through and do what we're able. When working on an activity gets tough, it's okay to pause and give ourselves little brain breaks. These short, positive distractions can help us recharge and accomplish more. God often uses such moments to refuel us and to inspire us.

Prayer

Lord, be in charge of all my work—I depend completely on you to make it happen and to bring about my heart's desires. Amen.

DOING THE RIGHT THING

So, my dear children, don't let anyone divert you from the truth. It's the person who acts right who is right, just as we see it lived out in our righteous Messiah.
1 JOHN 3:7

Wouldn't it be great if doing the right thing was always easy and you never even had to think twice about it?

Sometimes doing the right thing causes anxiousness, especially as a teenager. As a Christian teen, you are faced with temptation left and right. Temptation doesn't always look extreme, like taking drugs. There are other subtle signs, like staying quiet when someone is being bullied; watching a show your parents told you not to watch; finding money and keeping it when it doesn't belong to you.

These moments are tests. God has already told us what he expects, but peer pressure and society can tempt us to do the opposite of what is good and right.

Then there are especially difficult situations when you're stuck deciding between two *rights*, like two good friends hashing through a tough argument. Who do you side with when you can find grace and wisdom in both of their points? Has this ever happened to you? How did you handle the situation?

No matter what problem or issue you are dealing with, God's hand is there to guide you. When you pray and seek God about what you should do, he will guide you to do the right thing. Be brave—God blesses righteousness.

Anxiety Relief Activity

Decision Tree (page 166). Doing the right thing or making the best choice may not always be clear when your thoughts keep running around in your head. Make a decision tree, and write down all the options, including possible outcomes. This often makes decision-making easier. Even though you recently did this activity, it's a skill that, once learned, helps many people make beneficial choices throughout their lives. Practice this activity again so you'll always remember how to do it.

Prayer

God, please make my path clear and give me the strength to make choices that are pleasing to you. Amen.

GOD'S PROTECTION

The fear of human opinion disables; trusting in God protects you from that.

PROVERBS 29:25

You might not actively follow the news, but social media makes sure we know what's going on in the world—without giving us much control over what we see and when. One minute we're enjoying the content on our feed, and the next, tragic stories are filling the screen.

Taking in distressing information can impact our moods and ability to function. For instance, being scared to go outside makes perfect sense when the media only focuses on showing frightening realities. While it's important to know what's happening around the world, it may not always be a good time to consume that information. "Trusting in God protects you." A decade from now, when you look back on your teen years, you'll want to have good memories, like simply having fun and enjoying being young with fewer responsibilities. Limit your consumption of tragic news and human opinions about worldly events. Trust that God always works to do good, even in bad situations, and find something that makes you feel happy and uplifted.

Anxiety Relief Activity

Body Scan (page 124). When we experience anxiety, our bodies alert us in different ways. By completing a mental body scan from the bottoms of our feet to the top of our heads, we learn how and what our bodies are communicating to us. By becoming practiced at body scans, we can learn to recognize and tend to our early symptoms.

Prayer

God, this world can be scary. Thank you for giving protection and peace to me and to all who love you. Amen.

FROM AVOIDANCE TO AUTHORITY

Even when the way goes through Death Valley, I'm not afraid when you walk at my side. Your trusty shepherd's crook makes me feel secure.
PSALM 23:4

Avoiding your fears might seem like the easiest and best solution, because your anxiety convinces you that you simply cannot face what is challenging you. The problem with avoiding your fears is that it's only a temporary solution.

You can't put off hard tasks or conversations forever. One teacher might let you skip your presentation when you explain to her that you're too nervous, but not every teacher may be as understanding.

Sometimes putting something off for too long can have negative results when you finally confront it. You might avoid submitting scholarship applications because you're scared of rejection, but the longer you put it off, the less time you have to do your best in preparing the application to submit by the deadline.

You have to walk through the shadows—"Death Valley"—to get to the light at the end of the tunnel. But you're not alone. God is with you even in the darkest, scariest times, to make you feel secure. You can do it.

Anxiety Relief Activity

Gradual Exposure (page 148). It might feel more comfortable to wait until all your fear is gone before you resume normal life, but that won't always leave you feeling satisfied. Gradually immersing and exposing yourself to what you're afraid of or that stirs anxiety in you can help you confront challenges with confidence and ultimately build confidence and trust in yourself. This activity will help you move forward while also maintaining a sense of control.

Prayer

Father, you are with me, even when the path ahead leads to scary places. Thank you for staying at my side. Amen.

NEVER TOO YOUNG

Don't let anyone put you down because you're young. Teach believers with your life: by word, by demeanor, by love, by faith, by integrity.
1 TIMOTHY 4:12

This is one of my favorite Bible verses. It advocates for young people to take on big challenges, and it energizes them to make huge changes in the world. I felt a calling from a young age to help other young people, but I sensed that others, including adults, didn't take me seriously because of my age. This made me question my gifts and abilities at trying to make a difference at that age.

Young people can make mature decisions, but some adults might think they're not ready yet. Even you might feel you're too young to use your spiritual gifts and abilities in the big ways God intends for you.

You can do big things! It's never too early for God to use you. What are your passions? What are your big dreams? You are not too young to make your goals come to life. Jesus was only 12 years old when he spoke with religious leaders and impressed them with all he knew.

If you don't feel ready or aren't sure where God is leading you yet, that's okay! As you find your own path, you can "teach believers with your life: by word, by demeanor, by love, by faith, by integrity." This means if you are gracious, kind, loving, full of faith in God, and honest and reliable, you're ready for God to use you to bless people.

You only need to be willing.

Anxiety Relief Activity

Positive Affirmations (page 152). Affirmations are positive truths you repeat to yourself. They pump you up and remind you of who you are and what you're capable of doing. Affirmations can help relieve your anxiety and doubts.

Prayer

God, I know you can use me, even at my young age. Help me be courageous as you show me how to be a blessing. Amen.

STEPPING FORWARD DESPITE FEAR

"I, your God, have a firm grip on you and I'm not letting go. I'm telling you, 'Don't panic. I'm right here to help you.'"
ISAIAH 41:13

What does it mean when God says, "Don't panic. I'm right here to help you"? Does that mean you'll never experience fear or anxiety again? Since we are still human, we'll continue to experience a range of emotions, including frustration, sadness, and fear.

What the verse means is that you're not alone, because God has a firm grip on you—he's holding your hand. It also means that when you don't feel strong, he'll strengthen you. You'll be able to continue forward, even if you're scared, because God's not letting go of you.

Running for class president but nervous about having to speak in front of your classmates? It's okay. You have God walking with you every step of the way.

Let God's amazing statement sink into your heart: "I'm right here to help you." You can find peace in knowing that God is with you and will help you through any situation you face.

Rising Above: Teen Devotional for Girls

One mantra I hold on to is, "Do it scared," because if I wait until I'm not scared at all, I may never do it. But I can do it scared because God is right there with me.

And he is with you too. Will you trust him to help you?

Anxiety Relief Activity

Breathe In Confidence, Breathe Out Fear (page 162). This activity might still sound strange, but trust me. Mindful breathing will help bring you back to your body and senses and can be an excellent tool to help you feel more confident. With that building confidence and also God at your side, you can step forward, despite any fear.

Prayer

God, thank you for being right here with me, holding my hand. Help me do what I need to do, even when I'm scared. Amen.

FOLLOW YOUR PASSIONATE HEART

So, what do you think? With God on our side like this, how can we lose?
ROMANS 8:31

Maybe you feel this, too, but I get anxious about things I'm most passionate about. Do issues like world hunger, changes in your school, or activities like planning a protest or church event you are passionate about give you anxiety? What gifts and talents are you most passionate and proud of?

I'm passionate about helping parents and teens build better relationships together, and supporting teens to develop skills to better their mental health is important to me. I never want parents or guardians to feel upset or judged, but sometimes I feel anxious when I have to relay a tough message. But my job is to be the best advocate for teens like you, so you can be heard and understood by the adults around you.

Teens are some of the most passionate and aware individuals on this planet. They challenge adults to question traditions and thinking that may be harmful. Young people are bold in standing up for what they believe is right. You all have some of the biggest hearts this world will ever see.

You might wonder if you're too young to make a mark on your neighborhood, your community, or even the world, or if it's too much to ask, or if anyone even cares. But like Romans 8:31 says, "With God on our side like this, how can we lose?" If God is leading you to make a difference, he will help you to achieve his purposes. Your anxiety does not have to stop you. Let it fuel you instead.

Anxiety Relief Activity

Speak to Your Inner Child (page 134). Some people struggling with anxiety had childhood experiences that made them feel unsafe. Some remember the event that caused their insecurity, but don't realize that the incident caused ongoing feelings of anxiety. During your teen years, these types of experiences may not yet be clear to you. Talk with your inner child, who might still feel unsafe. Help them to feel secure and protected. When you do, some of your feelings of anxiety may fade as a result.

Prayer

Father, thank you for the desires of my heart that you've given me. Bless me with peace and strength to move forward to achieve them. Amen.

BRIGHT PATH AHEAD

Now you've got my feet on the life path, all radiant from the shining of your face. Ever since you took my hand, I'm on the right way.
PSALM 16:11

We know life is a roller coaster. But having anxiety during those roller coasters? The worst! As if life isn't hard enough on its own, anxiety comes and makes everything harder. When you're on a roller coaster, everyone reacts differently: Some scream during the scariest turns, a few even panic. Some close their eyes, while others choose to watch what's coming next.

In life we have the same choices: be so scared that you keep your eyes and hearts tightly closed, or open your eyes and see that, even though it's scary right now and your adrenaline is going, there are some really beautiful sights around you and just ahead.

The path God has laid out ahead of you is shining brightly—"radiant"—with his presence. You might not know exactly when God will place you there or where it will lead. It's okay to not have everything figured out yet. And it's okay to trust where God is taking you. Life is to be lived and enjoyed, not dreaded and feared. With God at your side, one day it will be wondrous.

Anxiety Relief Activity

Conquering Intrusive Thoughts (page 144). Sneaky, intrusive thoughts try to prove us wrong about ourselves and pull us off God's path for us. You can conquer intrusive thoughts by stopping them and choosing to think the opposite. For instance, if you're thinking, *What if I fail?* conquer that by thinking, *What if I succeed?* Free up your imagination to come up with ideas that can launch you toward much better outcomes, outcomes that God intends.

Prayer

God, help me be less consumed with worry and fear so I can enjoy my journey and this life that you blessed me with. Amen.

WORRIED ABOUT THE FUTURE? FOCUS ON TODAY

"Give your entire attention to what God is doing right now, and don't get worked up about what may or may not happen tomorrow. God will help you deal with whatever hard things come up when the time comes."
MATTHEW 6:34

This Scripture makes anxiety sound like an easy thing to kick, right? But it's not easy. Anxiety makes you worry about things that make no sense. You may find yourself going down a rabbit hole of thoughts, freaking yourself out about things that likely will never happen. You're pulled into an endless sequence of what-ifs, which triggers more anxiety. *What if I don't make it? What if everyone laughs at me? What if I fail?*

Worrying doesn't make a problem go away. Worrying consumes your mind and takes away joy. Worrying keeps you from seeing what God is doing around you.

When you realize you're having anxious thoughts, it's important to rein them in. Focus on now, not tomorrow. What can you do now, in this moment, to accomplish today's goals? Once you have the answer, just do the next one thing. Then do the next one thing. You can do this, even if the task is not your favorite, even if it's only one tiny accomplishment at a time. Soon, you may see that you can handle many more of life's events than you realized.

"God will help you deal with" the hard stuff. He promises to.

Anxiety Relief Activity

Reframing Thoughts (page 146). Some negative thoughts about ourselves may be partially true, but negativity limits our confidence and ability to do or be more than what we currently believe. Worse, we can get stuck because of our fear of failure. But we can change our perspectives by reframing those negative thoughts to include positive statements and goals. This inspires the mind to find ways to push forward and achieve more. It also makes it easier to deal with challenging situations.

Prayer

Lord, help me focus on today and not worry about tomorrow. Thank you for promising to always help me with the hard stuff. Amen.

GOD BLESSES YOU TO BE READY FOR ANYTHING

God can pour on the blessings in astonishing ways so that you're ready for anything and everything.
2 CORINTHIANS 9:8

Many young people I work with struggle with anxiety. Some worry about themselves, their families, and what might happen. Especially with COVID-19, the uncertainties seem big and endless. Some feared that their parents would lose their jobs, while others worried about having to move in with other family members to save money.

Many young people fear an unknown future.

And yet, God assures us we don't need to.

No matter what your anxiety tells you, God will provide. In fact, "God can pour on the blessings in astonishing ways." That means you'll have food to eat. Clothes to wear. A place to sleep. People in your life who care about you. Because God loves to bless. He pours on the blessings! So, he will make sure that you have what you need.

Life brings changes, new circumstances, and uncertainty. Many of us worry over these unknowns. But God already has plans to care and provide for us, no matter what comes.

Worrying won't make a situation change, but trusting that God will make a way can bring blessings of calm and readiness for any changes in life. Can you recall a time you felt worried about something, prayed, and then felt God's reassurance?

Anxiety Relief Activity

5 Senses, or 5-4-3-2-1 (page 122). When your anxiety and emotions are on overload, and even if you're dissociating, this simple activity will guide you to use your five senses to help calm you and bring your mind and body back into reality. You should then feel more grounded and think more clearly. You might even be able to look around and see where God has poured on the blessings.

Prayer

God, I release all of my worries to you. I believe you will always provide everything I need at the right time. Amen.

WHEN NOTHING SEEMS CERTAIN, JESUS IS CONSTANT

For Jesus doesn't change—yesterday, today, tomorrow, he's always totally himself.
HEBREWS 13:8

Change is hard for any teenager, but fear of the unknown can heighten anxiety. Maybe your family or home is changing. Your parents may be getting divorced, you might be moving to a new town, or a parent could be bringing a new child into the family. Not knowing what will happen after the change is the scariest part.

All kinds of questions can start to overwhelm you. *How will I spend time with both of my parents? Will my parents be okay not being together? Will my friends forget me when I move?*

Changes happen every day and are a part of life, and it doesn't always get easier to adjust to unexpected turns. But most often, life eventually settles into a new normal that is no longer scary.

Jesus Christ (*Christ* means king) will never change. He will always be there for you—always loving, always caring. That's who he is, and "he's always totally himself." When everything around you seems to be moving and you don't have any control, Jesus is your anchor. All you need to do is talk to him in prayer, and he is there.

Anxiety Relief Activity

Audio Journaling (page 142). Try speaking your thoughts into the voice notes on your phone or other device. You might start venting or talking about negative feelings you're experiencing. We're often made to feel that we shouldn't say our negative thoughts aloud, but sometimes we need to hear ourselves to realize how anxious we are or how ridiculously hard we're being on ourselves. After the negative, speak some positive truths about yourself or the situation.

Prayer

Jesus, thank you for being the unchanging constant in my life! Thank you for being my anchor when everything else in life feels unstable. Amen.

YOUR ANXIETY WILL BE GONE

God met me more than halfway, he freed me from my anxious fears.
PSALM 34:4

What would your life look like if you were free of anxiety? All of it. Gone. Visualize it. How might your relationships look different? What would your grades look like? How would you operate through life if you weren't consumed with worry about what might go wrong?

You may have cried out, like me, for God to just take away the anxiety so life can feel easier. You might have heard others say you just need to have more faith. Or maybe you felt that God could help you at one point, but now you feel differently. It's okay.

God hears you and cares about all your worries, no matter where you are in your faith. God does not love you any less if you have doubts. And having doubts definitely does not mean that you've lost your faith forever.

We all have different faith journeys, and God knows and understands. He is still there for you. Remember, we give grace to ourselves, just as God gives us grace. He can and will free you from this weight.

Anxiety Relief Activity

Brain Break (page 170). While God is working to grow our faith and bring about his plans for us, we still have our responsibilities and daily tasks to do. And we may still feel fear or stress when doing them. Part of giving ourselves grace includes pausing everyday activities and taking brain breaks when we need to. These short, positive distractions can help us to recharge and then keep going so we accomplish more. God often uses such moments to ease our fears and to inspire us.

Prayer

God, help my faith in you to grow so I can rest knowing you will deliver me from my fears. Amen.

NO SIN TOO GREAT TO FORGIVE

Because of the sacrifice of the Messiah, his blood poured out on the altar of the cross, we're a free people—free of penalties and punishments chalked up by all our misdeeds. And not just barely free, either. Abundantly free!
EPHESIANS 1:7

When we really want to please God but feel we keep messing up, these setbacks can really take a toll on our mental space. When we've sinned, we might feel unworthy and unlovable. *Have I sinned too much? Can God really forgive me? Is what I did too bad?*

Forgiveness is a promise that God has given us, and with forgiveness, we have freedom from penalties. "And not just barely free, either. Abundantly free!" God is gracious, merciful, and loving. Jesus' redeeming blood was shed so that we can receive complete grace and forgiveness.

Your anxiety might try to convince you that you don't deserve forgiveness, that what you've done is "too bad." But remember that anxious thoughts are based on fears of what *could* happen, not facts.

We will all make mistakes in the future. We are human and mistakes happen. No, we shouldn't go out and purposely make mistakes just because God is gracious. But we also shouldn't beat ourselves up over our mistakes. God forgives—that is a fact.

You are still worthy. You are still very loved. So, free your mind of worry over forgiveness. Your loving Father wants you abundantly free.

Anxiety Relief Activity

Change Your Environment (page 158). Creating a space can be inspiring or relaxing. It can be a place to spend time with God—reading the Bible, praying, and being assured of his forgiveness and healing. If you already have a special space, add to it or change it up. No matter how you're feeling, you'll have a designated space just for you . . . and God.

Prayer

God, I am so grateful for your redeeming blood that is forgiving, gracious, merciful, and loving. Thank you for staying close to me. Amen.

STRONGER THAN YOU THINK

*My dear children, you come from God and belong to God. You have
already won a big victory . . . for the Spirit in you is far stronger than
anything in the world.*

1 JOHN 4:4

The Holy Spirit dwelling within you—and you being in Christ—
makes you so much stronger than you could ever imagine. God
already made you so strong, so courageous. But with him filling
you and empowering you? Setbacks can only be temporary.
They don't stand a chance.

Even when you feel that your strength is depleted and empty,
you are still empowered, because he is within you. Just like the
verse says, "the Spirit in you is far stronger than anything in
the world."

God is greater than anything you will ever face in the world.
Even now, as a teenager, with God's Spirit in you, you are an
overcomer.

You can do this—whatever it is that you are feeling challenged
by. God promises to always take care of you and to be right
there with you, no matter what. Take that thought with you this
week: *God is bigger and stronger than anything I will ever face.*

Always hold firmly to God. He is good.

Anxiety Relief Activity

Gradual Muscle Relaxation (page 126). Stress stores itself in your body and will make parts of your body stiff and tense. Muscle relaxation not only relaxes your body, but it'll help ease your mind as well. God designed relaxed muscles to repair themselves so they (the body and the mind) can grow stronger.

Prayer

Lord, thank you for teaching me how to get stronger. Thank you for being bigger and stronger than anything I'll ever face. Amen.

LET YOUR SPIRIT SING

May God himself, the God who makes everything holy and whole, make you holy and whole, put you together—spirit, soul, and body—and keep you fit for the coming of our Master, Jesus Christ.
1 THESSALONIANS 5:23

Some of our anxieties and fears are physical—we're afraid of the impact a person or incident might have on our physical bodies or we care about how we're seen by others and want to feel accepted.

For instance, you might be worried about not having the right clothes and feeling embarrassed or judged and rejected by others.

However, we must remember that we are, at the core, spiritual beings. Our spirits are the batteries that power us. They're the life force. So when fear and anxiety drain us, we need to recharge our whole selves, including our batteries. Our spirits.

Only God can actually recharge a person's spirit, so we need to draw close to him. "God himself . . . makes everything holy and whole." We draw close by immersing ourselves in the Bible, in prayer (God is *so* close to you in both!), and even by listening and singing along to our favorite Christian music. Nothing we can do is more uplifting to our hearts. And when we lift our hearts to God, he will uplift our spirits.

So immerse yourself in the Bible and prayer, and let your voice, your heart, and your spirit sing. God, in his infinite love, will recharge your battery, putting you "together—spirit, soul, and body."

Anxiety Relief Activity

Connect with Your Love Language (page 154). Discovering and responding to your love language can fill a void of love that your heart and spirit may feel is missing. It's one of the best ways to help yourself feel loved—and to help your spirit sing.

Prayer

Lord, help me regularly meet you in the Bible, prayer, and in song. And when I do, recharge all of me, body and spirit. Amen.

GOD'S PLAN AND PURPOSE FOR YOU

Job answered God: "I'm convinced: You can do anything and everything. Nothing and no one can upset your plans."
JOB 42:1–2

When I was in high school, one of our youth leaders thought it would be a great idea for me to participate in the local oratorical contest. The rules: write your own speech and perform it from memory. The writing part? Easy! Reciting it from memory? Not so much. The leader was convinced I would do a great job as a speaker because of my academic skills, so I gave it a shot. Somehow, they convinced me to participate three years in a row. And each time, it was awful! I froze and forgot lines I wrote, *every single year!*

I wish I could tell you that I eventually won the contest. I didn't. But I'll tell you what did happen: I now make a living by speaking to the public, and that includes speaking to crowds. Wild, right? You know what's even more wild? I love doing it.

Just because something that you do now brings up lots of anxiety in you doesn't mean you aren't capable of achieving it. Is there something in your life that you're working toward but you're challenged by it? If you love something, keep working on it. It may be part of God's plan for your life ahead.

Anxiety Relief Activity

Belly Breaths (page 138). If you're having a panic attack, the first line of defense is to slow your breathing with belly breaths. Regulating your breathing will send a message to your brain that you are safe. The second line of defense is to secure yourself. After belly breathing, use the "5 Senses, or 5-4-3-2-1" technique (page 122) to help bring your mind and body back into reality. The third line of defense is to trust God's plan for your day, your week, and your life.

Prayer

Lord, thank you for your plan for my life. Thank you that you will help me achieve it . . . and even love it. Amen.

FREE YOURSELF FROM PERFECTION

"Are you tired? Worn out? . . . Come to me. Get away with me and you'll recover your life. I'll show you how to take a real rest. Walk with me and work with me—watch how I do it. Learn the unforced rhythms of grace. I won't lay anything heavy or ill-fitting on you."
MATTHEW 11:28–29

Sometimes the pressure we put on ourselves can cause anxiety.

Maybe we put that pressure on ourselves because of the way we are being raised, or it's because we push ourselves for excellence. But when we think about excellence, what we really want is *perfection*. Anxiety kicks in when we feel we're not perfect enough.

When we get into this mode, there are two common results. One, we can end up *underperforming*. We spend more time stressing and overthinking what we need to complete the task perfectly than actually completing it. This stress can sometimes look like crying, pacing, or panic attacks. We might avoid by procrastinating, sleeping, or doing other activities to distract ourselves.

Two, while in perfection mode, we tend to *drive ourselves into exhaustion*. We overdo it and tire ourselves out. When we're exhausted, we get cranky and snap at people who don't deserve it. We burn out, so we're not able to put any energy into areas that we love. We can even make ourselves sick.

God wants you to perform well, but he also wants you to take care of yourself. Even Jesus rested when he needed it. He lovingly encourages you to take good care of your body, mind, energy, responsibilities, and others.

Anxiety Relief Activity

Get Moving (page 128). Know when to rest, and know when to get moving again. When you have anxiety or when you're sluggish, moving your body—even in a small way—can start you going forward to complete your tasks.

Prayer

God, please free me from perfectionism. Thank you for encouraging me to rest and for inviting me to walk and work with you. Amen.

PERFECTLY IMPERFECT

Keep company with God, get in on the best.
PSALM 37:4

You can easily fall down the path of perfectionism, when all you really want is to succeed. Did you know that attempting to do everything perfectly can be a trap into anxiety?

Feeling the need to be perfect might come from trying to please others, like family members or teachers, or you might even be putting the pressure on yourself. The desire to perform well isn't a bad thing, except when it begins to impede on the rest of your life.

I came across a video on social media, of a student who learned he was in the running to be valedictorian of his senior class. Leading up to graduation, he went into full competitive mode to make sure he would be the one to receive the title. And he did it. But, as he later reflected, he lost out on the last memories of high school with his friends, because he was so focused on getting to give a "five-minute speech" on graduation day.

Remember that God is proud of all your efforts, even if they're not perfect, so you don't need to overdo it. Find balance and, with it, peace. God wants to fulfill your heart's desires, and you don't have to miss out on amazing experiences to get them. Life is meant to be lived and enjoyed.

Anxiety Relief Activity

Brain Dump (page 130). Dumping all your thoughts on paper will help you discover your priorities. This will free you to find balance and peace.

Prayer

God, guide me. I want to achieve my heart's desires and also have plenty of time to enjoy the life you've blessed me with. Amen.

A JOYOUS FUTURE AWAITS

"I know what I'm doing. I have it all planned out—plans to take care of you, not abandon you, plans to give you the future you hope for."
JEREMIAH 29:11

You already know that a major part of anxiety is worrying about what might happen in the future. What college will you get into? Will you get married and live happily ever after? Are you doing enough for God? Are you making the right decisions about the future you want? The questions are endless.

Just as the questions are endless, so are God's promises for you. God promises, "I have it all planned out—plans to take care of you, not abandon you, plans to give you the future you hope for."

It's so comforting to know that he thinks about the years ahead of us, because, in our anxiety, so much of our future feels unexpected and uncertain in the here and now. This verse reminds us that God has always had a plan for us to have happiness and success.

God's plan is one that you can trust. You can't always trust anxious thoughts, but you can trust that God will lead you into a bright future. Keep today's Bible verse close to your heart. God himself will ensure that you, his precious child, will find joy.

Anxiety Relief Activity

Create a Vision Board (page 168). A vision board is simply a poster board of glued-on pictures that show what you want to achieve in the future. As I mentioned, I prefer using glue and paper so I can see it on my wall daily, but you could also create a digital vision board using programs such as Canva or Google Slides. From time to time, create a new vision board and place it on your wall to keep your newest dreams and goals in mind. This can help you stay focused on your goals (and God's goals) and help you achieve them.

Prayer

God, thank you for your future plans for me, plans of hope and joy—and that you'll be with me always, just as you are now. Amen.

Part 2

Anxiety Relief Activities

Create an Anxiety-Attack Safety Plan

USEFUL FOR: managing anxiety and panic attacks
TIME: 10–15 minutes

A safety plan is a tool for when your symptoms become more difficult to manage.

Anxiety attacks can be scary, and in that moment, you might have trouble recalling the coping skills from this book that are particularly helpful to you. Creating a safety plan to keep with you will give you a list of coping skills to use in case you struggle to remember them during an anxiety attack.

1. On a piece of paper, write across the top: *My symptoms during an anxiety attack.*

2. Beneath that, list five physical and mental symptoms that occur during your anxiety or panic attacks. (For example, pounding heart, trembling. Search online if you need help identifying your symptoms.)

3. Next, add the most common *triggers* (causes) that start your anxiety attacks, such as yelling or loud noises. (If your triggers are listed on your safety plan, someone helping you might identify why the attack started and possibly move you away from the source.)

4. Beneath that, write: *What helps me.*

5. List coping skills that are typically the most helpful when you're having an anxious experience. Some ideas might

include taking a walk, drinking water, listening to music, and coloring. (As you discover the activities in this book, you might add a few of them to your safety plan, along with a few reminders of how to do them.) If one or more Bible verses are helpful and meaningful to you, add those too.

6. List three people you (or someone helping you) can contact when you're struggling. For each of the three people, write their first name, phone number(s), and relationship to you. If you have a therapist, ask them about adding their contact information to your safety plan as well.

7. Having this list with you at all times will be helpful if you come into contact with someone during your anxiety attack and they aren't sure what's happening or how to respond. (This list of symptoms will also be beneficial if you seek professional help with managing your anxiety.)

8. A safety plan can be helpful for people close to you. If you have frequent anxiety attacks, you may want to share your plan with a couple of people you trust, like a parent or relative, a school counselor, and/or a friend.

TIP: During an anxiety attack, it may be helpful to start by contacting one of your safe people who has a copy of your safety plan. They can walk you through using your skills and support you as you bring your anxiety levels back down.

5 Senses, or 5-4-3-2-1

USEFUL FOR: dissociation, poor concentration, sensory sensitivity
TIME: 1–2 minutes

Anxiety can make your mind feel detached from your body and your surroundings. This is known as *dissociation*. Anxiety can also make it difficult to concentrate.

This activity can help your mind and body return to the present moment, and help soothe your anxious symptoms.

1. Sit or lie comfortably, if you can. (This activity will still work if you can't get comfortable, like if you're at a pep rally that might be causing anxious feelings.)

2. Focus your attention on the room or space you're physically in, *or* use your mind to envision a peaceful place, like a seashore.

3. Identify five things you can see. (If you choose a beach for your peaceful place, you might visualize the ocean, sand, palm trees, beach towels, and flip-flops.)

4. Identify four things you can feel. (On the beach you might feel the warm sun, a nice breeze, your swimsuit, and sand between your toes.)

5. Now, it's time for three things you hear. (At the ocean, you might hear waves rolling in, seagulls calling, and children playing in the water.)

6. What are two things you can smell? (Do you smell the salty ocean? Seafood smells coming from a restaurant near the beach?)

7. Lastly, what is one thing you can taste? (Maybe you brought a nice cold lemonade with you, and you can taste the tangy lemons.)

TIP:

- If you envision a peaceful place, you might experience greater relief to envision Jesus there with you.

- You may feel even more grounded (less detached) if you write down the 5-4-3-2-1 objects you identify.

- It may be helpful to remember that the numbers decrease according to how difficult it may be to identify items. For instance, finding five items to *see* is easier than the number of things you can *smell* or *taste*. That is why those are listed last. Be aware that what you see or envision may very well be blessings from God.

Body Scan

USEFUL FOR: recognizing where your body holds tension, relaxing
TIME: 5 minutes

Different feelings or signs in your body can signal to you that you might be getting anxious or stressed. For example, when your legs start shaking or your heart beats faster. Or the signs might be more subtle, like your jaw clenching or your toes curling.

As you pay closer attention to the ways your body communicates with you, you'll be able to choose an activity to help you manage anxious responses more quickly. This will prevent bigger responses, like panic attacks.

1. Sit or lie comfortably. It's okay if you aren't completely comfortable; you'll start to feel more relaxed as you go through the scan.

2. Take several slow, deep breaths.

3. Start with your focus at the top of your head. Does your head feel pressure? Does your mind feel cloudy? If so, pause there. *Breathe slowly and deeply. Relax the area as best you can. Envision the tension or fogginess leaving.*

4. Move your attention down to your neck and shoulders. Do you feel any tension there? If so, pause there. *Breathe slowly and deeply. Relax the area as best you can. Envision the*

tension leaving. (Stay in each area of your body for as long as needed to encourage more relaxation.)

5. Bring your attention down to your arms, elbows, and into your hands and fingertips. Any tension here? Slowly continue the scan and relaxation techniques toward your feet.

6. Next, focus on your back. Your bottom and the backs of your thighs and legs. Your ankles and feet. Your shins and knees. Your thighs and hips. Your belly. Your chest and heart. (If your heart is beating fast, spend more time here, with more slow, deep breaths.)

7. As you move up, notice any tension in your face. Are you clenching or grinding your teeth? Are your eyebrows tight and frowning? Do you feel any sensations in your nose and ears?

8. Observe how each area of your body holds tension. For each tense area, breathe slowly and deeply. Relax the area as best you can. Envision the tension leaving.

9. After you become familiar with the activity, you'll recognize how your body uniquely communicates tension, stress, and anxiety. When you notice similar physical reactions in the future, pause and relax the areas to help you manage anxious responses before they become disruptive.

TIP: If you struggle to keep focus, imagine a feather resting or Jesus' warm, comforting light soothing each area of tension.

Gradual Muscle Relaxation

USEFUL FOR: releasing tension in the body, regaining strength
TIME: 5 minutes

Similar to the body scan, in this activity you'll engage your whole body to release stress and anxiety.

During gradual muscle relaxation, you'll pay attention to muscle groups, one at a time, tensing and releasing them as you inhale and exhale.

This is an activity you can do daily. You could even do this in your seat at school with no one knowing that you're doing anything. It's also one of the best ways to relax your body in bed when you can't fall asleep.

1. Sit or lie comfortably. If lying down, rest on your back with your arms and legs uncrossed.

2. Starting with your feet, inhale deeply as you tighten the muscles in your toes and feet. Hold them that way for a few seconds, then relax them and exhale fully.

3. Moving up from your feet, focus on your calves. Inhale deeply, tighten the muscles, hold for a few seconds, then relax and exhale fully.

4. Do the same for your thighs and then your abdomen. Inhale deeply, tighten the muscles, hold for a few seconds, then relax and exhale fully.

5. Shift your focus to your hands and arms. Clench your fists, then tighten the muscles in your forearms, and then your upper arms. For each muscle group, inhale deeply, tighten the muscles, hold for a few seconds, then relax and exhale fully.

6. Next, focus on your shoulders, then your neck, and then your face (including mouth, nose, eyes, and eyebrows). For each muscle group, inhale deeply, tighten the muscles, hold for a few seconds, then relax and exhale fully.

TIP:

• Take your time with this activity. You may get better results if you close your eyes and think of soothing sounds, such as ocean waves. Or listen to a recording of nature sounds. God intentionally created many nature sounds to be calming.

• Muscle relaxation not only relaxes your body, it helps ease your mind as well. God designed relaxed muscles to repair themselves so they (the body and the mind) can all grow healthier and stronger.

Get Moving

USEFUL FOR: when you can't seem to shake those anxious feelings; easing out of fight, flight, or freeze stress responses; when you're sluggish and need to start moving again
TIME: 3–30 minutes

When you have anxiety you can't get rid of, *or* you feel your body beginning a fight, flight, or freeze response to an intensely stressful person or situation, *or* you need to simply get yourself going again, then moving your body can help ease the stress or sluggishness out of you.

This will allow you to get to a safe place or to complete your tasks.

1. If you're frozen in place or tempted to run, gain control over yourself with small movements such as:

    -   shifting your head,
    -   running your hand up or down your thigh, or
    -   twisting your foot from side to side.

    After that small, first movement, you'll be better able to keep moving. Then you can walk away and get safe or find a place to be by yourself.

2. Practice this every time you start to experience a fight, flight, or freeze response. Soon, freeing yourself of the physical response will become easier and quicker to do.

3. If you're not frozen in place or tempted to run, take a break from the source of stress. Whether it's homework, work, or an intense conversation making you feel overwhelmed, ask to take a break. Find a place to be by yourself.

4. For either scenario 1 or 2, the next step is to identity a movement activity that will take you at least a few minutes to do and get you active. For example, taking a walk, dancing, yoga, or stretching.

5. Set a timer for five minutes. Setting a timer will remind you that you'll return to your previous activity shortly, or that you'll begin an activity.

6. Move (walk, dance, yoga, stretch) for five minutes. (If you need to restart the timer, that is perfectly fine.) If possible, have fun with it. Let yourself feel the stress and tension leaving your body. This will help you keep moving.

TIP: When possible, pick an activity that you enjoy, that excites you, or that brings you peace. Also, be open to trying other movement activities. You might not usually be a dancer, but let loose and try it anyway. Again, try to have as much fun with this activity as you can. Laughter (fun) is the best medicine (BTW, that saying originated in the Bible, in Proverbs 17:22—"A cheerful disposition is good for your health").

Brain Dump

USEFUL FOR: managing busy thoughts, discovering priorities
TIME: 5 minutes

Have you ever had so much to do or think about that it was difficult to tell one thought from another? Or maybe you couldn't figure out your priorities? Brain dumping is useful for getting all of your thoughts and tasks out of your head and onto paper so you can process and do them more easily.

Responding to the mental swirl of tasks and priorities one by one will be much easier than attempting to address them all at once or under pressure.

1. On a piece of paper, list all your thoughts, including the tasks you have to do, that are swimming through your head.

2. Don't try to put them in any order yet. Just write them down as they come. (If you have trouble doing even this, take a moment to pray and ask God to help you. He will.)

3. Next, organize the to-do tasks from most important to least important. Or, if importance doesn't matter, organize them according to how much time each task will take.

4. Try starting with the task that will take the least amount of time. By starting with a simple task, you get your brain into gear to complete bigger tasks.

5. Next, do you need to solve any of the to-do tasks right now? If so, start doing the tasks that you can resolve through action. (Actions might include asking someone to help you.)

6. Go down your list of things you need to do now, tackling one item at a time.

7. Later, when you have more time, go back to your brain dump list and journal (write your observations and ideas) about any other thoughts you would like to process.

TIP: If one or more tasks on your list has several steps, it might be helpful to brainstorm and break down the steps needed for each one. Writing out the action steps can make it feel easier to do. Try not to overdo it and prioritize instead.

Journal Your Feelings

USEFUL FOR: expressing your feelings, clearing your mind
TIME: 5 minutes

Sometimes we struggle to understand and express our feelings. Daily journaling is a helpful way to process our emotions, whether the emotions are from today or from years ago.

Writing out your feelings and the events surrounding them can help provide relief and healing, whether you journal about positive or negative feelings.

1. Pick a time of day to journal.

2. If you choose to journal in the mornings, start by writing about the previous day. This can help you get your day off to a better start. If you journal in the evenings, you can process the events that happened throughout the day. (You can try both times of day and see which one works better for you.) Journaling can be helpful at any time of day, even if it's writing a short note about how you feel each day.

3. Grab a notebook and a pen. (It's helpful to have a notebook just for journaling your emotions.)

4. Start writing whatever comes to mind about your emotions and the situation that caused them. Try not to correct too much or try to make your words sound the "right" way. Just let the words flow.

5. If it would help ease your heart, try starting your journal entries as "letters to God" or "Dear Jesus."

6. After writing about your emotions, end with a few words of gratitude—a couple of blessings you're grateful for right now.

7. Finally, make a few notes about your intentions for how you want to move forward regarding what you wrote about.

8. Once each month, reflect back on that month's journal entries. Once each year, page back through the year's entries. Looking back can remind you of how many issues you have resolved and how much you have overcome.

TIP: Some journals that you can purchase come with helpful prompts. Look in stores or online for creative journal prompts that will help kick-start your writing flow.

Speak to Your Inner Child

USEFUL FOR: everyday anxious feelings, when you're worried about something that'll happen in your day
TIME: 10 minutes

Your inner child is the part of you that holds your memories. When you have anxious thoughts and aren't sure why, it could be because of a negative experience that your inner child remembers that you may not consciously recall.

Speaking to your inner child gives you the opportunity to care for the younger version of yourself in a way that the adults in your life might not have known you needed.

1. Find a place to be alone.

2. Sit comfortably. You're going to talk to your anxious or upset inner child.

3. What is the child's name? (You can use your actual name, if you'd like.) How old are they? What do you remember about how you looked as a child? (Visualizing details can make this activity easier.)

4. Pause to think about what your inner child might be feeling right now. Identify the emotion. Is it fear? Disappointment?

5. Can you identify the very first time you felt the same overwhelming emotion as a child? (This may be a time when you had a strong emotional reaction to a situation, but couldn't communicate your emotions at that age. So, that emotion

was never acknowledged, and the child was not helped to feel better or safer.)

6. If you need help remembering, pray. It might sound too simple, but God wants you healed and whole.

7. Speak to your frightened inner child with gentleness and kindness. Acknowledge what they are feeling, without judgment. Help them feel safe and then encourage them.

TIP: Try using this technique if you're nervous about an upcoming tough conversation you need to have. Identify the very first time you felt a similar emotion. Say something like, "I understand when you felt _____ (insert negative emotion) before. I know you're nervous now about this upcoming conversation, but I promise to keep you safe. No matter what they say, we're going to be okay."

Speak to a Therapist

USEFUL FOR: managing anxiety and everyday stress
TIME: 1 hour per week, for however long you'd like to talk with a therapist

Speaking with a therapist is not something that you can do once and your anxiety magically vanishes. Seeing results from therapy takes time, and it's important to develop a trusting relationship with the right counselor, usually a minimum of four weeks.

Everyone's process with therapy looks different, and the thought of talking to a stranger about your life and feelings can be scary. This activity provides tips on how to prepare for your first therapy session.

1. Be prepared to answer a lot of questions. The first session, typically called an intake session, is for the therapist to gather background information on you, your family, and why you might be seeking services. Remember, there is no right or wrong answer.

2. Be as honest and open as possible. Don't feel rushed or impatient if it takes time to get comfortable opening up. When you allow yourself to be comfortable, you might find that your sessions are more open, honest, and effective in return.

3. Put in the effort to complete activities they recommend after your sessions. I know, homework, especially outside of

school, can sound tedious and boring, but practice reinforces what you learn in your therapy sessions.

TIP:

- Therapy is not always an easy process. Sometimes you might feel like your emotions are getting more intense. It just means you are becoming more aware of your emotions and making progress. Trust the process and know that your therapist is there to be a valuable addition to your support system.

- How would someone find a good therapist? Many cities and towns have community mental health agencies that offer services for free, charge based on a person's income, or use a person's health insurance. Websites with therapist resources (like psychologytoday.com, therapyforblackgirls.com, nami .org, teencounseling.com, or my own, notesbykhia.com) have lists of therapists in your area, and you can check patient reviews, find what the therapists' specialties are, and see how they charge for services. You can also call 211 and receive public community resources as well. More and more therapists offer virtual therapy services, making it easier to meet with them. If there are a limited number of therapists in your area, you can also speak with your school counselor. Different states have different rules about the age that a young person can start therapy on their own. Most places will require a parent's permission and information.

Belly Breaths

USEFUL FOR: gaining control of your emotions
TIME: 1 minute

When you're experiencing high levels of stress, you may notice your breathing getting faster and shallower, or sometimes you might forget to breathe at all. Breathing is one thing you can control, even when you feel out of control.

Focusing on your breath will help you slow down and manage stressful situations much more calmly.

1. Take a deep breath in through your nose, counting slowly to four. As you slowly inhale, bring your attention to your stomach, and notice it inflate and expand outward.

2. Hold your breath for two seconds.

3. Breathe out through your mouth, counting slowly to four. You should feel your heart rate decrease and your stomach deflate.

4. Again, breathe in through your nose for four, stomach inflating, hold for two, breathe out through your mouth for four. Repeat these deep breathing steps as many times as you need to, until you feel your emotions easing and your body beginning to relax.

TIP:

- Do this activity slowly, step by step. Going too fast will only increase your heart rate, then the activity will not be as effective.

- You may find it helpful to have a playlist of your favorite soothing Christian songs for times when you need to calm yourself or to play in the background while you do this activity. The songs can also help you remember that God is right there with you and he has good, good plans for you, now and in the future.

Sit with Your Emotions

USEFUL FOR: heavy emotional days, days when you're unsure why you're feeling emotional, everyday anxious feelings
TIME: 2–5 minutes

Sometimes it's helpful to sit still and listen for what our emotions may be attempting to say to us. When we take the time to sit with these emotions, without judgment or stopping them, our unconscious and subconscious thoughts and feelings can be revealed, showing us where the anxiety may be stemming from.

1. Find a place to be alone.

2. Sit or lie comfortably. (I prefer to do this on the floor.) Take several slow, deep breaths.

3. Allow your body and mind to feel all the emotions that come up. Don't try to interrupt them. (If you feel yourself start to cry, don't try to stop the tears from flowing. Let it happen.)

4. Allow yourself to feel everything before you start following the next steps to soothe yourself.

5. Thoughts will likely start to come into your mind about how you feel. Stick with those thoughts. You might experience thoughts like, *This is too much; I am so overwhelmed.*

6. Allow all of those thoughts to come out, along with the emotional responses they might bring, such as crying or screaming.

7. After you let those emotions out by feeling, crying, or screaming, you should notice your body beginning to relax.

8. Use your journal (or a dedicated notebook as a journal) to process these experiences and determine your next steps from a calmer state of being.

TIP:

- You may feel the instinct to stop the emotions and hold back from letting your feelings out through crying, screaming, or other emotional expressions. Those emotional expressions mean you have a lot of heavy feelings stored in your body and need to be released.

- Express those intense emotions, *freely* crying, screaming, or however they want to come out without hurting yourself or others around you.

- With practice, you may find yourself assessing your anxious thoughts and feelings more quickly and accurately.

- Try looking up an emotion wheel online to help identify specific emotions.

Audio Journaling

Recording your thoughts onto your phone or another device can be a great alternative to the typical way of journaling. (This is also an option if you're concerned that someone may read your journal.)

This activity can be useful when you have so much on your mind that you're struggling to sleep, or if you're preparing to have a difficult conversation with someone.

1. Grab your phone or another device with recording capabilities.

2. Use the video recording option or the audio recording app.

3. Start speaking your thoughts aloud into your device.

4. Record without starting over, criticizing your voice, or thinking too much about your words.

5. After you've finished, think about the thoughts and feelings you expressed and meditate on them. Did you say anything that surprised you? Did you express any feelings you weren't aware you had? If you spoke a lot of negative, either about a situation or about yourself, finish up by recording some positive truths, particularly about yourself. After all, you are a child of the King. Finally, speak words to remind yourself that Jesus will always be your steady anchor during life's storms.

6. Create a plan of action steps to change any of these thoughts or feelings that you have. Even if your plan is to move forward and "let it go," that is still a plan of action.

TIP: Try not to think too hard during this activity. Your recording doesn't have to be grammatically correct, and the words don't need to be perfect. Do your best to just let the words flow as they come out. And be sure to include positive truths.

Conquering Intrusive Thoughts

USEFUL FOR: intrusive thoughts
TIME: 1 minute

Intrusive thoughts are negative thoughts that unintentionally come to our minds. These thoughts can disrupt our days, impact the way we view ourselves, and increase feelings of anxiety.

Anxiety may be provoking the thought. So might the Enemy. It's certainly not coming from God, who loves you.

This activity will help you stop those thoughts in their tracks and shift them from negative to positive—from untrue to true. When you consistently challenge negative thoughts with positive ones, you'll become more confident and better able to conquer the challenges of the day.

1. Acknowledge that the negative thought is there. *That's a negative thought.*

2. Interrupt the thought with, *I know that's not true.*

3. Write down the negative thought. (It's helpful to keep a list of your intrusive thoughts in a notebook that's reserved just for this purpose.)

4. Identify the opposite of the negative thought. If the thought was, *I can't do this*, an opposite would be, *I can do this*.

5. Write down the opposite of the negative thought in your intrusive-thoughts notebook. This further reinforces the positive thought.

6. Identify a fact that proves the negative thought is false. If the thought is, *I can't do this*, remind yourself of a time when you were able to do the same thing, something similar, or even something else you thought you couldn't do. *I thought I couldn't* _____ (fill in with something you had doubts about in the past), *and I did it*.

7. Write down the fact or memory that proves the negative thought is false.

8. Verbalize the positive thought. "I can do this."

TIP:

• When you're doing your best to think more positively, you initially might feel frustrated that these negative thoughts still intrude. Remember to be kind to yourself through this process. These thoughts are called intrusive for a reason: they are not wanted. If needed, take some deep breaths, and then continue the positive thoughts.

• As you consistently put this activity into practice, you'll quickly be able to recognize—and conquer—negative, intrusive thoughts.

Reframing Thoughts

USEFUL FOR: intrusive thoughts, self-doubt
TIME: 1 minute

Sometimes our intrusive thoughts are true to a certain extent. For example: *I'm not good at taking tests.* Though that may be partially true, the way we think about ourselves and our current circumstances have a big impact on how the experiences unfold.

We can reframe our thoughts by changing the perspective. Then we'll have the power to change the reality of the statement.

1. Acknowledge the thought. For example, *I'm not good at taking tests.* (It may be true that tests cause anxious feelings and make it difficult to concentrate or recall what you've learned.)

2. Reframe the thought. Instead of, *I'm not good at taking tests,* you can restate it in a more positive way. *I've struggled with taking tests in the past.* (Thinking that you *aren't* good at taking tests mentally eliminates the possibility of improvement. By reframing that thought, you open your mind to recognize that a better outcome is possible.)

3. Add an "and" statement to the end of the thought: *I've struggled with taking tests in the past,* **and** *I'm working to increase my test-taking skills.* By adding the "and"

statement to your thought, you're acknowledging your efforts and reminding yourself that your circumstances can, in fact, improve!

TIP: When you find yourself interrupting your thoughts or statements with "but," try changing the "but" to "and." By changing the conjunction to "and," you're recognizing both sides of your thoughts and feelings. Instead of *I really want to beat my track speed record,* **but** *I can't seem to do it,* try, *I really want to beat my track speed record,* **and** *I'm determined to keep practicing until I do.*

Gradual Exposure

USEFUL FOR: taking your time getting acquainted with something that makes you fearful, helping you feel more peaceful
TIME: one week

Have you ever had a task to complete that seemed too overwhelming to do all at once, but you knew it had to be done eventually? (Like a school project to complete but you felt anxious when you tried to work on it.)

In this activity, acknowledge the fear and anxiety you feel in your body *and* conquer them at the same time—at your own pace. This activity is designed to help you see that you can regain control of your body and responses, even when you feel completely out of control in a particular situation. This activity can help to bring peace.

1. Identify one fear that you'll focus on conquering this week. For example, studying for a big test coming up. (Conquering too many fears at once can be overwhelming.)

2. Set a timer for 15 minutes. (Setting a timer reminds you that you don't have to do this for too long.)

3. Start the activity. For example, to begin studying for a test, maybe read over some of your notes for 15 minutes.

4. Once the timer stops, reward yourself. Enjoy a healthy snack or a quick activity, like listening to your favorite song or getting fresh air. Take a break for 5 or 10 minutes.

5. Start again for another 15 minutes before taking another short break.

6. Gradually increase the time by 5- or 10-minute increments. (Try to reach 30 minutes, with 10-minute breaks in between.) It's okay to adjust and scale back.

7. Repeat as many times as you need throughout the day and week until the project is complete. Or until you're able to face the fear without the anxious responses.

TIP:

- For tasks with a deadline, practice shorter breaks in between (5-minute breaks). For tasks without deadlines, try once a day.

- God is gentle and patient with you, so be gentle and patient with yourself.

Visualization Brings Better Outcomes

USEFUL FOR: focusing on positive outcomes
TIME: 3–5 minutes

When we're preparing for a big event, we can experience excitement and nervousness at the same time. Maybe you're getting ready to accept an award or meet with a college recruiter. This is a great opportunity, and it can also simultaneously feel overwhelming.

Visualizing the good experiences that you want to have during the event can help you focus more on the positive possibilities than the negative. This can train your brain to bring about positive perspectives that can help fuel better outcomes during the event—which is likely what God has planned.

1. Sit or lie comfortably. Close your eyes, if you'd like.

2. Visualize yourself at the event. What are you wearing? Who is with you? What do your surroundings look like? Visualize yourself walking smoothly and with confidence.

3. Think of the positive emotions you will feel. Are you excited? How proud of yourself are you? Are you smiling? Imagine how confident you will feel.

4. Allow all of the positive emotions to take over your body for a full minute or more. It's okay to smile and feel joy.

5. Now, when the event happens in real life, your brain will recall those positive thoughts and feelings. If you experience any

anxiety before the event, bring that visualization back to mind. Consistently doing this before events and meetings can result in more and more positive outcomes.

TIP: While practicing this activity, it may be helpful to turn on soothing music to help you focus.

Positive Affirmations

USEFUL FOR: self-confidence, easing everyday anxieties
TIME: 1 minute

When you feel anxious, you might have negative thoughts about yourself or your abilities. To challenge those thoughts, write positive affirmations—words that support and encourage yourself. Later, reflect on your affirmations to help change anxiety into confidence.

1. There are a few different ways to create and use your affirmations. Here are three good examples you can try. Feel free to do any and all that work well for you.

   - Write your affirmations down on individual pieces of paper that you can easily hang on your wall or mirror. You can use small note cards, colorful sticky notes, or any pieces of unlined paper you have.

   - Carry a small notebook with you. If you begin to have a negative thought, quickly write the opposite of that thought in the notebook—tell yourself the positive truth.

   - Write down one to three affirmations (*I am smart. I am funny. I am beautiful/stylish. I can do this. God is with me. I will do well in my upcoming speech.*) and place them in your pocket or bag at the beginning of your day. If you experience any anxiety during the day, pull out an affirmation and meditate on it.

TIP:

- If you have a hard time creating affirmations, use Scripture. You could use a verse like Psalm 139:14: "I thank you, High God—you're breathtaking! Body and soul, I am marvelously made! I worship in adoration—what a creation!"

- Another verse that may be helpful is Philippians 4:13: "Whatever I have, wherever I am, I can make it through anything in the One who makes me who I am."

Connect with Your Love Language

USEFUL FOR: when you need to feel a little extra love and care, when you need to feel spiritually uplifted
TIME: 5 minutes

There are five *love languages*—five different ways that most people feel love—that author Gary Chapman, PhD, identified and made popular in his best-selling book. The five love languages are physical touch, quality time, words of affirmation, receiving gifts, and acts of service.

When your love language(s) haven't been tapped into in a while, you might find yourself feeling irritable, overwhelmed, or sad. You can help yourself to feel loved by doing the activity below.

1. Take a "love language" test online. Your results will show you the percentages of each of the five that apply to you. In other words, they'll reveal your main love language(s).

2. Identify ways you can show love to yourself, based on your main love language(s). Here are some suggestions for each one.

   • **Physical Touch:** Give yourself a big hug or hug a loved one. You can also warm up your hands and massage your arms, and even your legs, in a warm, comforting way.

   • **Quality Time:** Ask a good friend to come over and hang out for a while. Grab your favorite snacks and enjoy some of your favorite activities.

- **Acts of Service:** Make your favorite snack or meal. Reorganize your room in a new way that you'll enjoy.
- **Words of Affirmation:** Write some positive, uplifting affirmations to yourself and hang them where you'll see them.
- **Gifts:** Get yourself a little something nice.

TIP:

- It's okay to ask others for help. If you can meet your own needs, you will gain confidence knowing that you understand yourself. You can also show support to your loved ones by learning their love language and making them feel special and cared for.

- Discovering and responding to your love language is one of the best ways to help yourself feel loved and uplifted.

Creative Expression

USEFUL FOR: brain breaks, daily symptom management, satisfaction with oneself, comfort

TIME: varies

We often think of creative expression as formal artistic expressions like painting, drawing, or writing poetry, and those are good examples. But the truth is, anything you put your heart into can be a creative expression.

Expressing your feelings in an artistic way is especially helpful if you struggle to find the words.

The repetitive movements involved in your creative expression may also be relaxing to you. Best of all, this activity might even help you discover some new special abilities.

1. Explore some creative avenues that you enjoy, such as painting, drawing, or writing poetry. Do you like music? Try writing a song, a rap, or playing an instrument. Try belting out your favorite song. Do you like making jewelry? String beads to make a new bracelet. Like to play basketball? Get creative with your shots or your alley-oops. Enjoy cooking? Try a new recipe.

2. Whatever creative pursuit makes your heart happy and relaxes you, take a little time and enjoy it each day. Some days you may be able to enjoy it for a few minutes. Other days, you can have fun with it for a couple of hours or longer.

TIP: You don't have to be perfect (or even good) at the activity of your choice. This activity is not a talent show. It's an outlet meant to safely express yourself and to release any tension you may have in your body that's causing an anxious response. Don't worry about how good the end result is. Just go for it. You might even find a talent that you didn't realize you had, or a hobby you didn't imagine might interest you.After all, God delights in surprising us.

Change Your Environment

USEFUL FOR: creating a safe and comfortable environment for yourself, creating a special space where you can connect with God

TIME: varies

You aren't able to control every environment that you step into, but you can make a space for yourself that's as comforting and peaceful as possible.

When you have anxious feelings and aren't able to find reprieve, get into this space that you'll design.

1. Choose a space to convert. This can be your whole room, part of a room, or even a closet.

2. Gather items that make you feel comfortable and safe. You might want to add pillows, different lighting, a candle, and a speaker for playing relaxing music. (You can add little trinkets that are special to you to make it uniquely yours, a little at a time.)

3. Add some inspiration. This might be a good space for colorful sticky notes with comforting Bible verses, maybe from Psalms.

4. Use the space when you journal, speak to your inner child, complete body scans, or just want to feel comfortable and safe.

TIP:

- The space you create does not have to be large. Even if you share a room with a family member, you can use a small part of the room for your peaceful corner.

- If you aren't able to transform a space, you can still create positive environments for yourself. For example, when you need to relax, you can make the bathroom your safe space and take a relaxing bath or shower.

- Your space can also be a place where you spend time with God—reading the Bible, praying, and being assured of his forgiveness and healing.

Heart Hug

USEFUL FOR: increased heart rate, anxiety attacks
TIME: 1 minute

You might notice your heart beating faster when you're in an anxiety-provoking situation. Or you might simply need to feel that someone is hugging you when no one is able to. You can reduce some of the anxiety you feel by slowing your heart rate. And you can feel hugged, even when you're alone.

Since you can't reach in and take hold of your heart, you can give it a hug from the outside.

1. Place your right hand on your chest where you can feel your heart beating. Place your left hand on your stomach.

2. Gently but firmly, press your right hand on your chest. At the same time, press your left hand up under your ribs—again, gently but firmly.

3. Imagine your heart as a tiny little box that's holding all of your anxious feelings, and that it's beating so fast because it's scared.

4. Visualize yourself holding your heart in your hands. Reassure it that it's safe. Think comforting thoughts to it. *You're safe, little heart. I've got you.*

5. Still pressing your hands around your heart, take a deep breath in through your nose, counting slowly to four. Hold your breath for two seconds. Then breathe out through your

mouth, counting slowly to four. Release all of those anxious feelings while you breathe out.

6. Repeat the deep-breathing steps a couple of times, until you feel your heart and body begin to relax and your mind begin to clear.

TIP: Don't be afraid to press firmly up under your rib cage with your left hand. Think of this as a warm, tight hug. If possible, also get a hug from a trusted loved one who makes you feel safe and cared for.

Breathe In Confidence, Breathe Out Fear

USEFUL FOR: when you're facing a big challenge
TIME: 1 minute

If you're feeling nervous about a big challenge you're about to face, such as public speaking, taking your driver's test, or having a difficult conversation, you can use your breathing and your body to increase your confidence.

This activity calls for your mind and body to work together.

1. Either stand or sit up tall with your feet planted firmly on the floor. Think about pushing all of your weight to the floor. It may be helpful to close your eyes, if you can.

2. Focus your attention on the bottoms of your feet as you get ready to take a big, deep breath in through your nose.

3. Think to yourself, *Breathe in confidence*, as you inhale, and visualize confidence flowing in from the bottoms of your feet, all the way up your body.

4. You can imagine confidence as a color, but really get a picture of confidence filling your body.

5. Think to yourself, *Breathe out fear*, as you exhale, and picture fear being pushed out of your body in every direction. Envision confidence forcing out the fear.

6. You can imagine fear as smoke or steam, but get a picture of fear leaving your body.

7. Start again from the bottoms of your feet. Continue a few more times, until you feel little or no nervousness and are ready to take on the challenge.

TIP: Remember to breathe slowly and intentionally. Before you start each round, pause and pray for God to help ease your nerves.

Set Healthy Boundaries

USEFUL FOR: creating healthy relationships, decreasing anxiety-provoking interactions
TIME: varies

What does it mean to *set boundaries*? It means deciding what you will and will not stand for, when it comes to your life and your interactions with others.

Setting boundaries for your life may look like deciding to limit the amount of time you spend on social media, if it's causing you anxiety or keeping you from doing your homework or chores.

It's not always comfortable to set boundaries, and enforcing them can be even more uncomfortable. But setting a boundary usually causes less anxiety than not having a protective boundary at all.

1. Establish the boundary and why it is necessary. (For example, *Only 30 minutes of social media per day so that I get my work done.* Ending conversations when someone starts to gossip with you.)

2. When we don't have a clear boundary—and reason and rules for it—then it's more likely we won't hold ourselves to it.

3. Practice stating out loud what your boundaries are, and how you will respond if the lines are crossed. (For example, "I do

not feel comfortable talking about people behind their back. Let's change the subject.")

TIP: Having boundaries could result in relationships changing or ending, and that can be hard. Talk to someone you trust before or after. Tell them how you feel about the loss or change. It may help ease the discomfort.

Decision Tree

USEFUL FOR: being confident in your ability to make decisions, building trust in yourself
TIME: 5 minutes

When you're faced with an important decision, anxious feelings can arise. Creating a decision tree can help you see your options more clearly. As you do this activity, ask and listen for the Holy Spirit's guidance.

1. At the top of a piece of paper, write the decision you have to make. For example, "Whether or not to accept the job offer."

2. Write the influencing factors underneath in the form of questions to yourself, starting with the most important factor. So, if it's most important to you to have a job at the mall, write, "Is the job at the mall?" (Your next questions might be whether you would like the work, will they be flexible with your school schedule, and will they allow you time off for family time or church.) You get the idea. Write down all the influencing factors you can think of.

3. In the left margin of the paper, halfway down the page, write "no," and in the right margin of the paper, halfway down the page, write "yes."

4. Draw a line from each influencing factor to your response, whether it's yes or no.

5. To make your decision, reflect on the questions you answered "yes."

TIP:

- When you're making a decision about something that's positive, doesn't go against God's will, and isn't going to cause anyone harm, there is no such thing as a "bad" or "wrong" decision—it's just a decision. Whatever you decide will be great or you'll learn a lot of beneficial lessons from it.

- Reading the Bible regularly will help you to hear the Holy Spirit's leading and also teach you to make good decisions. Try reading for just a few minutes every day. Psalms might be a good place to start.

Create a Vision Board

USEFUL FOR: building confidence, helping you stay focused on your goals and future plans

TIME: 1 hour

A *vision board* is a visual representation of what you want and inspiration for you to achieve it. It's a poster board filled with pictures of goals and dreams that you want to reach (such as graduation or getting your own car).

This board serves as a daily reminder of what you want and why you want it, which will help you remain focused if you begin to doubt yourself.

The board can focus on one goal or contain many goals.

1. Get a poster board, like one you might use for a school project; pick any color that you enjoy. You'll also need glue and colored pens or slim colored markers to write with. (Optional items include stickers, glitter, and other fun decorations.)

2. Gather pictures of what you want to achieve or earn. (If the Holy Spirit reveals to you his plans for your future, add those too.) Some people like to cut pictures out of magazines. I like to get my pictures from the internet because I can find specific images.

3. Prepare to glue everything to the board. Come up with a layout, and leave room to write your goals and inspiring quotes. Then glue the pictures to the board.

4. Add words. Use quotes and write out your desires. Make sure the words you use are specific. If you want to end the year with 10 scholarship offers, write that on the board.

5. If you like, decorate your vision board with stickers and glitter, and add any visuals that make you feel good or inspired.

6. Hang the finished board in a place where you'll see it every day. Avoid putting it behind doors. Keep it out in the open.

7. Reflect on the board often to remind yourself of your goals. Ask God to help you achieve them.

TIP:

- Have fun with this activity. Invite friends to join you to create their own vision boards, turn on your favorite songs, and be as creative as you want to be *or* keep it simple. This is your board and your dreams.

- Create a new vision board every year, or as soon as you achieve the goals on your current vision board.

- I prefer using glue and paper so I can see it on my wall daily, but you may choose to create your vision board on a computer using a program like Canva or Google Slides. You can even save it as your computer's background or screen saver so it is always in your view.

Brain Break

USEFUL FOR: when your mind needs a break
TIME: varies

Have you ever been working so hard on a project that your thoughts seem to turn to mush? Your brain might be signaling to you that it needs a little break. Even Jesus took breaks, usually on a mountain or in a boat.

For this activity, choose an uplifting and easy distraction that doesn't take much brain power. Choose a distraction that can temporarily pull your mind and attention away from your work.

1. Set a timer for 10 to 20 minutes. (The timer will make sure you don't get too distracted from the original project.)

2. Pick an activity. Would you like to take a nap or rest for a short while? Get a snack or something to drink? Go for a short walk outdoors? Pet your dog or cat? Read a chapter from a book? Color or draw? Play a short computer game, like sudoku? The activity should be something that you enjoy and will help you relax.

TIP:

- If the project is due the next morning, you may want to take a shorter brain break, such as five minutes.

- For projects with a due date further out, you may be able to take a brain break up to half an hour, or return to it the next day.

Acknowledgments

To my sisters, Kambré and Kalyn. Thank you for listening to me and encouraging me when I doubted myself on this project. Thank you for your many insights, and for helping me recall anxious situations we had as teenagers. You are incredible women. I am so proud to be your big sister.

Aria and Kenya, thank you for sharing your struggles with me as you move from your teen years and into adulthood. I have enjoyed watching both of you grow up. I am so excited to see what more God has planned for you.

My therapist, Karyll, your patience and our work together helped me so much in completing this book. You have been a rock for me the past couple of years. You have helped me understand myself better and identify my anxious thoughts and feelings. With your support and on top of my formal training, I was able to complete this with an entirely different perspective and level of understanding. I am grateful for you.

To my friends, who respected my privacy when I couldn't tell you many details about this project but encouraged me anyway. Your kindness did not go unnoticed.

Last, but not least, my parents—SURPRISE! I really wanted this to be a surprise for you. Imagining your responses kept me energized to complete this book.

References

American Psychiatric Association. *Diagnostic and Statistical Manual of Mental Disorders, Fifth Edition, Text Revision.* Washington, DC: American Psychiatric Publishing, Inc., 2013.

Chapman, Gary. *The 5 Love Languages: The Secret to Love That Lasts*, Reprint edition. Chicago: Northfield Publishing, 2015.

Galanti, Regine. *Anxiety Relief for Teens: Essential CBT Skills and Mindfulness Practices to Overcome Anxiety and Stress.* New York: Zeitgeist Young Adult, 2020.

Goldstein, Esther. "What Is an Inner Child and What Does It Know?" *Integrative Psychotherapy* (blog). April 6, 2021. https://IntegrativePsych.co/new-blog/what-is-an-inner-child.

About the Author

 Khia Glover, LCSW, is a therapist and mental health coach who specializes in working with children and BIPOC communities.

Khia's work as a school-based therapist and school social worker has given her a front-row seat to the emerging needs of children.

She started her company, Notes by Khia, in response to the mental health struggles she witnessed in her professional work with children of all ages, as well as her own mental health struggles, both in childhood and adulthood.

Notes by Khia is a mental health education platform that offers a variety of services for individuals, families, and large groups. One of her primary focuses is leading children and families to regain optimal mental health. She does this by teaching parents and professionals who work with minority children and families mindful skills that will provide children the safest and most nurturing environment for success.

Khia is dedicated to providing a safe space for her clients to express themselves authentically and to receive the support they need to manage their stressors so they can begin to live a life of peace and wellness.

Visit her website, notesbykhia.com, or connect with her on Instagram, TikTok, and Twitter @notesbykhia.

Hi there,

We hope *Rising Above: Teen Devotional for Girls* helped you. If you have any questions or concerns about your book, or have received a damaged copy, please contact customerservice@penguinrandomhouse.com. We're here and happy to help.

Also, please consider writing a review on your favorite retailer's website to let others know what you thought of the book.

Sincerely,
The Zeitgeist Team